CLEANING AND CARING FOR BOOKS

Peter Gibson

CLEANING AND CARING FOR BOOKS

A Practical Manual by
ROBERT L. SHEP

LONDON: SHEPPARD PRESS

First published in the United States of America in 1980
under the title CLEANING AND REPAIRING BOOKS
Revised and expanded edition first published in Britain
under the present title, 1982

© ROBERT L. SHEP, 1982

I.S.B.N.: Card Cover, 0 900661 24 9
Cased, cloth covered boards, 0 900661 25 7

SHEPPARD PRESS LIMITED
P.O. BOX 42, RUSSELL CHAMBERS, COVENT GARDEN
LONDON WC2E 8AX

Printed for the Publishers by Nene Litho
and bound by Woolnough Bookbinding

CONTENTS

Foreword 7
Parts of a Book 11
Tools & Supplies + Some Sources 12
Techniques 22
Problems and How to Deal with Them 37
Replacing Flyleaves 67
Maintaining Your Library 78
Repairing Books for Libraries 87
"Don'ts" — A Review Section 92
Packing & Posting Books 94
Further Reading 97
Index 98

ILLUSTRATIONS by MARTHA FUREY

1. The Parts of a Book 10
2. Book Press 15
3. Cutting Knife 16
4. Cracked Hinge 31
5. Folding a Corner Protector 57
6. Tears in Pages 66
7. Tipping in a Flyleaf 69
8. Trimming a Flyleaf 71

THE AUTHOR

ROBERT L. SHEP is an American who studied in London and then lived for several years in England before returning to the United States where, for more than twenty years, he had been a dealer in secondhand and antiquarian books. During the whole of this time he has cleaned and repaired books, not only from his own purchases and stock, but also for local art museums and libraries. He teaches classes and runs training workshops in these subjects. His book is, therefore, the fruit of much practical experience.

FOREWORD

This is not a book on bookbinding, nor is it a technical book on the restoration and conservation of rare books. It does not in any way pretend to be.

This is a book for people who are interested in books and want their libraries to both look well and be in good repair. It should give them confidence to buy secondhand books, feeling that they will be able to clean them up and make them look presentable. It is also for book dealers who want to clean up their stock so that it is more salable, and need a guide to help them develop their skills in simple, everyday repairs, as well as a few more complicated ones.

What do you do, for example, when you get a book that proudly bears the message "Robin Smith age 8" scrawled in crayon on the inside of both covers? I think you shudder, but there are practical ways of dealing with this lapse of sanity.

My bookbinding teacher said that we should always leave names and dates in, as it would give a history of the book. I wondered about this until I found out that she was used to dealing with rare books belonging to famous people of the past. Clearly, she had not been faced with anything as devastating as "Robin Smith". I suppose I might add that I possess a first edition of Carl Sandburg's *Rootabaga Pigeons* that I was given at about age 4. I managed to deface it with crayons and tear out a few pages. I keep it both to remind me of the childhood friends that I find within its pages, and as an example of how not to treat a book.

What I have attempted to bring you is a number of different solutions (where possible) to problems that arise when cleaning and repairing books. You are urged to try these out on throwaway "practice" books, and then to use the methods that you find work for you. At the same time, it must be noted that each and every book is a situation unto itself. What methods you decide to use in tackling any problem must in the long run remain a matter of your personal judgement, based on how well you have developed your skills. In fact, you will find that the biggest decision you will have to make when confronted with some problems is whether or not to do anything about them at all; and that depends upon both your skills and the quality of the book you are dealing with.

I would sincerely urge anyone who has any great interest in the repair of books to seek out a course in Hand Bookbinding at your local college or crafts centre. Even if you feel that you do not want to get into this too deeply (for it can be very complicated), the knowledge you will gain about the construction of books is invaluable. It probably will not, however, teach you simple repairs and cleaning.

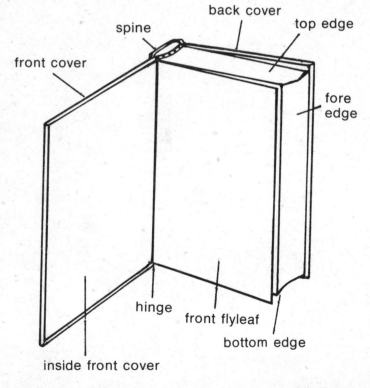

Parts of a Book

figure 1

PARTS OF A BOOK

There are a number of different terms used when describing the parts of a book. In order to avoid any confusion with terms you might already know, I am listing here the terms I will use so that we will all be talking about the same thing. Please refer to the illustration (facing).

1. Front Cover.
2. Inside Front Cover — the part of the Flyleaf (or endpaper) that is attached
3. Front Flyleaf or Free Flyleaf (or endpaper).
4. Bottom Edge — of the pages
5. Fore-edge (sometimes called Front Edge)
6. Top Edge
7. Back Cover
8. Spine (or outside spine)
9. Hinge — there is a front hinge and a back hinge (not shown)

These are most of the terms that I will be using, and I have given you a few of the alternatives that you might have heard elsewhere.

Another term is Dust Jacket or Dust Wrapper (d/w), which is the extra paper cover that goes on the outside of most hardbound books to keep the covers clean. Some better quality European paperbacks also have dust jackets.

TOOLS AND SUPPLIES

(*) indicates that a special note follows the list. All items are discussed in the body of the text.

Essentials

pencil rubber
sand paper — fine grades
waxed paper
blunt paring knife*
adhesive*
cleaning solvent*
rubber cement
old rags
dusting brush
transparent adhesive tape
brushes*
book plates — various
scissors
knitting needle

Additional Items

book press*
glue stick
liquid paper*
eraser stick (pink) with brush
renaissance wax
leather wax or preserver*
felt-tip pens, various (water colour)
water colour dyes
suede brush
rice paper – long fibre
commercial book cleaners*
label removers*
stretch bandage (old)

Items for Replacing Flyleaves

book press*
cutting knife*
book board scraps

steel ruler
folding bone
old telephone book

Blunt Paring Knife. I consider this my best friend when it comes to working on books. The one I have has a short blade, about 2½ to 3 inches long and it is stainless steel (which never holds an edge, anyway). I took it from the kitchen where its bluntness was not an asset, and now it won't cut anything, but it is wonderful for getting under things and a thousand other uses. I never fully realised how much I relied on my tools until I managed to mislay this knife. First I went crazy looking for it, and then I went out to the market and bought a new one. The new one is too sharp and feels different, and I don't like it at all. Meanwhile, my old one turned up just as I was beginning to despair, and I am feeling more attached to it than ever.

Adhesive. This can really be a problem if you do a lot of repair work. I used to use a white glue that dries transparent and works well with paper. The great advantage to it is that you can find it nearly anywhere and it comes in an applicator container that is really easy to work with.

If you do a lot of repair work, then you should really try to get something that is more flexible when it dries such as Spynflex or Laycock Flexible Glue. I now use a resin book paste, which I put into an applicator container for some work and in a wide-mouth jar for other jobs. I find this a very practical adhesive and it does a good job. The drawbacks are that I occasionally have to take the applicator off my container and run it under hot water until it is thoroughly cleaned out; and that it is hard to buy in small quantities.

Other types of adhesive you might want to consider are Dextrin pastes and various brands of plastic adhesives.

There is a paste you can make yourself for use with rice paper or gluing labels on, etc., and it is made as follows:

CORNFLOUR PASTE: 1 part cornflour
                    6 parts water

Cook this in a double boiler until it turns transparent, and then cook for 3 minutes longer. It has to be stored in the refrigerator and has a limited life. It does not have enough strength to be used to repair a cracked hinge or for other jobs of this type. It is possible to mix in one of the other, stronger, adhesives and this mixture will give you the strength you need.

A couple of drops of thymol can be added to the container of any of your adhesives to help prevent mildew in the book. Other mildew preventors can be found in a paint or wallpaper store.

Cleaning Solvent. What I actually use is carbon tetrachloride. There are also other products that can be used, one is Thawpit. Rubber cement thinner works pretty well for many things, but I do not like the odour. Someone suggested that I try lighter fluid for lifting off labels and it works pretty well, but I feel it might be dangerous and it seems to be a bit oily. I have often seen Hexane (petroleum ether B.P.) referred to for doing a number of jobs, but it is not easy to find. I use the spot remover (which I refer to as "cleaning fluid" out of force of habit) for most things, as it works well and there is very little chance that you can do any harm with it.

Brushes. It is good to have a variety of brushes around for various jobs, because not everything can be done with the same brush. I use three different types:

1. a watercolour brush, which is useful with dyes and various other small jobs;
2. an oil brush which I use for gluing jobs; the bristles are quite stiff and measure $\frac{1}{2}$" long and $\frac{3}{8}$" wide;
3. an all-nylon 1" housepaint brush for doing woodwork. I have cut the bristles down with a pair of scissors to a length of just under one inch to give me better control, and I use it to spread adhesive when I am replacing flyleaves.

It is very important that you keep all your brushes clean. Make certain that you wash them out and dry them after every use.

Liquid Paper. This is very handy if you use it intelligently. It comes in many shades now, and I usually keep white, ivory, and buff.

Book Press. (See illustration, fig. 2). I got along without a book press for almost eight years, and now I don't know how I did it. I finally saw one in a second hand store, decided that the price was right, and got it. Now I wish that I had two of them. If you are going to replace flyleaves, you really have to have one to get good pressure on the book. An old fashioned letter copying press, of the type that was common in offices, serves excellently.

Kafta, in *How to Clothbind a Paperback Book* (see FURTHER READING), tells how to make a substitute.

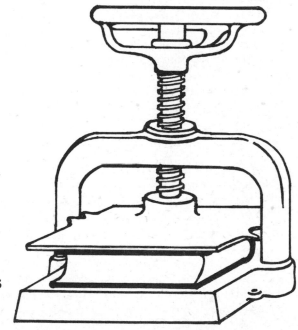

Book Press

figure 2

Cutting Knife. (See illustration, fig. 3). I only use this particular knife when I am replacing flyleaves, but then it is essential. It has to have a flat, narrow handle, and not a round one. The blades have to be replaceable and are razor sharp. They have to be replaced every so often, because it is very important that you get a good, clean cut each time. Several makes of trimmers or cutters with "snap-off blades" are now available at most artists supply stores and many general stationers.

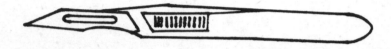

Cutting Knife   figure 3

Leather Wax and Preserver. There is always a lot of talk about what different people like in the way of products to use on leather. There are a lot of products available, and I will mention a few of them. There are a few more listed under Suppliers.

The British Museum puts out a leather dressing formula, which is:

Anhydrous lanoline	175g
Cedarwood oil	25ml
Beeswax	12g
Hexane (or Petroleum ether, BP 60°-80°)	270ml

Frankly, I find it very sticky.

Another formula often mentioned is:
50% neatsfoot oil
50% castor oil.

Some people recommend just plain vaseline. You might want to check with your local bindery to see if they have a good all-round leather dressing. I use Renaissance Wax.

Potassium lactate is recommended to clean and preserve leather. It will prevent rotting, but it will not cure it once it has started. I find that you can get a good leather preserver at many shoe stores, but I probably would not use it on a really valuable book until I had checked with a conservationist.

Commercial Book Cleaners. There are a number of products on the market. The one that I have got the most experience with is an Opaline Dry Cleaning Pad. This is for cleaning paper and I have found some limited use for it; you can usually buy it in an artists' supply store.

Label Removers. I have found three of these. One which you can get from Technical Library Service, is made for the purpose, and the other two called Stuart Stamp Lift and Instant Peel were made to take stamps off letters. This leads me to believe that you might find these and other similar products in stores that cater to stamp collectors.

SOURCES OF SUPPLY

Artists' Supply Stores. Good source for rice paper, brushes, knives, water colour dyes and many other items.

Jumble Sales. If you are near one, it is always worth looking for old paring knives, brushes, elastic bandages, etc.

Junk and Secondhand Shops. An especially good source for old book presses.

Pharmacies. A good pharmacy will usually stock a number of the chemicals that are mentioned in the text.

Shoe Repairers and Leather Goods Stores. Neatsfoot oil and leather waxes can be obtained from them, but try out patent brands on unimportant books before using them on any items of value.

Stationery and Office Supply Stores. You can turn up all sorts of new and interesting items in a good store. Always be very careful when using products for the first time, and test them out on practice books.

Some reputable suppliers whose products are well known and widely used have supplied the following details:

Edgar Backus Limited, 44-46 Cank Street, Leicester, LE1 5GU. Telephone: (0533) 58137.

BACKUS LEATHER BINDING POLISH, cleans and restores leather bindings. Sold in 500ml. tins (U.K. only).

BACKUS BOOKCLOTH CLEANER, restores and cleans buckram, linen, art and other bookcloths. Sold in 500ml. tins (U.K. only).

J. Hewit and Sons Limited, 97 Saint John Street, London EC1M 4AT. Telephone: (01) 253 6082.

LEATHER CLEANING AND PRESERVING DRESSING, a non-ionic synthetic wax with properties similar to beeswax. Sold in 500ml. bottles.

BOOKBINDERS' TOOLS AND SUPPLIES, adhesive (paste, glue, P.V.A.), bone folders, brass type and type holders, brushes, knives, papers (marbled etc.), presses, tapes, threads.

BINDING LEATHERS, basil, calf, goatskin, moroccos, pigskin, skivers, etc., in a wide range of colours.

BOOKCLOTHS, art canvas, buckram, linen, etc.

Hopkin and Williams, P.O. Box 1, Romford, Essex, RM1 1HA. Telephone: (01) 590-7700.

LEATHER DRESSING SOLUTION, made to British Museum formula. Sold in 500ml. tins, sufficient for treating about 200 average sized books.

POTASSIUM LACTATE SOLUTION, used to stabilise leather bindings against chemical decay. Sold in 500ml. packs, can be diluted with nine volumes of water to make solution for use.

Alfred Maltby and Son Limited, 28-30 Saint Michael's Street, Oxford OX1 2EB. Telephone: (0865) 43413.

FORTIFICUIR, Book leather dressing.

Arthur Rich and Partners Limited, 42 Mount Pleasant Drive, Belper, Derbyshire DE5 1AD. Telephone: (077 382) 3097. Royal Warrant Holders for the supply of Leather Dressings to H.M. the Queen.

PLIANTINE TRANSPARENT LEATHER PRESERVER AND DRESSING, a liquid to lubricate leather fibres and restore flexibility to old leather book bindings. 'Standard' for grain side (can be polished), 'Special' for flesh side of skin. Sold in 500ml. and in 1, 2.5 and 5 litre tins.

PLIANCREME LEATHER DRESSING CREAM a concentrated aqueous emulsion with same basic ingredients as Pliantine Standard with the addition of a fungicide. Not suitable for old books where water could have a detrimental effect on the leather. Sold in jars, 175g, 300g and 630g.

PLIANTEX CONSERVATION AGENT, an inert liquid which penetrates leather and on evaporation of the solvent leaves a clear film that protects individual fibres from further decay or spreading of the fungus that causes 'red rot', and gives support to any weakened structure. The film can be removed, if desired, even years later by a solvent. Sold in 500ml. and in 1, 2.5 and 5 litre tins.

Russell Bookcrafts, 94 Bancroft, Hitchin, Hertfordshire SG5 1NQ. Telephone: (0462) 59711. General suppliers to bookbinders, archivists and librarians.

DEACIDIFICATION. Materials for deacidification of books and documents by the vapour phase process using Cyclohexylamine Carbonate (C.H.C.) which neutralizes the acid in dry paper. Available in three forms: sachets of loose powder 10g, tablets, $\frac{1}{2}$g, and impregnated sheets of paper 10 x 8 ins. (254 x 203mm).

BOOKBINDERS' AND ARCHIVISTS' TOOLS AND SUPPLIES, fully equipped binders' benches, wooden and metal presses, adhesives (glue, paste, cold plastic etc.), agate burnishers, awls, bodkins, bone folders, British Museum formula dressing, sold in 85g. bottles, brushes, glass paper, guillotine, hemp, knives, shears, tapes.

BINDING LEATHERS, Oasis Nigerian goat, morocco, calf, white pigskin, sheepskin and skiver; parchment, vellum.

BOOKCLOTHS, BOARDS AND PAPERS (end and cover, including Cockerell hand-marbled, Ingres, Sylvia series etc.).

T. N. Waldron Limited, Avon Works, Stratford upon Avon, Warwickshire. Telephone: (0789) 292126. BOOK CORNERS. Corners of paper-covered metal to protect books in transit. Available in multiples of 100.

TECHNIQUES

You should start out by going to a charity shop or a jumble sale and asking if they have a couple of books that are so dilapidated that they are going to throw them away or sell them for almost nothing. If you do not want to do that, at least go through your own books and find a couple that you do not care about and are willing to make a lot of mistakes on.

All right, so now you have a book to work on. The next thing you have to do is look it over and determine just what might be done to make it more presentable and give it a longer life.

Let's suppose that we have found the following problems, most of which are very common, and marked them by placing strips of paper between the pages where they occur; leave the strips sticking out so you can find them easily:

1. price in pencil on the front flyleaf
2. name in ink on the inside cover
3. pencil markings inside the book
4. cracked hinge
5. top edge dusty
6. cover dull and faded

We are going to use these problems as a basis for beginning work. You will find many other problems listed in the chapter on PROBLEMS, but they should not be attempted until you feel that you have mastered the six listed above.

Before we go any farther, I would like to point out that you should take a very long-range view about books; they have a life of their own and any good book will probably survive you. You should develop a certain amount of respect for books, and any repairs you make should be able to be undone without damage to the book.

Going along with this thought, you should be careful and considerate when marking your books for identification. A neat, tasteful bookplate, or your name written in a corner of the inside front cover is one thing; scrawing your name in six different places in the book is an entirely different matter. Don't use a name embosser! If you are afraid that books will be borrowed and not returned, then it would be better not to lend them in the first place. In any case, the fact that you have defaced the book with your name all over it will not make any difference to someone who is either determined to keep it or who is too lazy to return it.

The most important point to consider when you are working with a book is whether you have the skill to tackle any given problem or whether it would be better for the book just to leave it alone. By using practice books, you will gain some measure of confidence in what you are capable of handling at this time. Then you will find that with practice you can build up your technique in the areas in which you are weak; or you might look for an alternative approach to the problem. You definitely should not try something on a good book if you have any doubts about the outcome. All these operations are skills, and these skills, like any other, have to be developed.

For example, it has taken me years to feel any confidence in removing bookplates. Usually, I just made a mess and then I felt bad about it; and I still don't do it unless I see no other choice. Even after doing a good job of removing a bookplate, the paper usually looks bad and I might have to put another bookplate in that space. If I have done a bad job of it and the paper of the flyleaf starts to come up, then I am faced with having to replace the entire flyleaf, and that usually means replacing the flyleaf at the other end of the book so that they match. Quite frankly, that is a lot of work. It would have been better for me just to have left the bookplate. If I didn't want the person's name in the book, I could have used one of the following ways to get rid of it: place another bookplate of the same size over it; sand the name off the bookplate: cover up the name with matching Liquid Paper.

As we go through these sample problems, I will try to point out some of the pitfalls as I see them, but most of all, you must learn to approach each job carefully and with a lot of patience, and you must learn to accept what can and cannot be done. You cannot make a used book look like a brand new one, but if you are careful, you could make it look a lot better than when you started to work on it, and that really is the whole point.

Going back to our sample problems, the first thing to do is realise that there is an order in which to work on them. On non-leather bindings, I work from the inside out to the cover. I also usually tackle all the small problems first, and then I try some of the bigger jobs last. On leather bindings, I always treat the cover first, and then go to the inside; but then I end up by treating the cover again when I finish up with the book.

Price in Pencil on Flyleaf

The first thing that probably comes to mind is that this is a very simple problem: "just erase it". I have been doing just that for about fifteen years, and the other day someone asked me a question while I was erasing a price. I stopped paying attention to what I was doing. The result was that I tore the flyleaf. Luckily, it was a very small tear and I fixed it with rice paper (see "Tears in Pages" in the chapter on PROBLEMS). Had it been worse, I would have had to replace the flyleaf.

Basically, erasing is not hard. I use a pencil rubber and keep several on my work table. You should develop the habit, in all operations, of working from the spine out towards the edges. You should never erase back and forth, like you see school children do, and which I used to do automatically until I trained myself out of it. Use short strokes, always in the same direction, and watch that you do not put too much pressure on the paper. Be especially careful on soft paper, as it will come up very easily.

Also be very careful of coloured paper, as a lot of it is not coloured all the way through, and even erasing will lift the colour off and leave you with a big white patch. You should approach any coloured paper very carefully, testing with small, light strokes to see if you can remove the pencil mark without removing the colour. This holds true for printed endpapers (the flyleaves) as well, as they will often react the same way.

Some people press down very hard when they write, and even after erasing you will have an impression in the paper. Often, you can lightly sand the area to rough up the paper a little (see the next section for details).

Name in Ink on Inside Cover

The first thing to remember when you are working on the inside cover is to support it from underneath so you do not crack the hinge. I usually put another, similar-sized book beneath the cover I am working on.

Ink is not as easy to deal with as pencil. Sometimes, a pencil rubber will take up ink, but not often. I do not like the grey erasers they make for removing ink, because they are harsh and I do not feel as if I have enough control when I use one, so usually do more harm than good.

Paper is a form of wood, and like wood it will react to sand paper. It has to be a very fine grade and you must be *very* careful, if you are not you can completely destroy the page with it. Therefore, some people never use sand paper, as they feel it is too harsh, and some people use it to good advantage with a great deal of caution. I keep small bits of sand paper in a jar on my work-table; they are of the finest grade I can find, and they are usually very well worn. I like to use pieces about two inches square. I wrap it around my thumb and hold it in place with my index finger. Use a very controlled motion, trying literally to lift the ink off the page. Again, as with an eraser, I use a very small stroke, working away from the spine towards the edge. When you are working on the inside cover, you have a bit more leeway, simply because that flyleaf is glued down. When you try the same thing on the free flyleaf, you really have to be careful. A good test is to hold the page up to the light to make sure you are not taking too much off. The type of paper will determine how far you can go. If you find you are creating a thin spot, STOP. I cannot stress too heavily that sanding is a difficult, tedious, and taxing skill, and until you feel very secure about your technique, you should not use it except in a practice book. Perhaps you never will use it, and that would not be so bad, either.

I really should have pointed out earlier that when you find names and signatures in books, you must determine whether or not you should leave them there. Obviously, in the case of "Robin age 8", there is no socially redeeming value in leaving it; but in the case of "Ben Franklin", it would be very undesirable to remove it. I was teaching someone to clean books and gave them a pile of books to work on, as they seemed very advanced in most of the basic techniques. Unfortunately, I had neglected to check over the pile first, and only too late remembered that one of them was signed by the author. My student had very carefully and neatly removed the signature. Needless to say, I was not amused. It is always wise to see just what names you have in your books, whether they are the author, or an important person in history or perhaps in the field that the book is about. The older a book is, the more chance you have of finding signatures of value.

Other ways of dealing with names that you do not want might be any of the following:

You can place a tasteful bookplate over the name. This is usually very easy to do; just make sure that you have it down neatly with no ripples in it. If you are applying it to the free flyleaf, don't wet it too much or it might make the paper pucker. Weighting the book down under large books or in a book press until the plate dries will help keep it smooth.

Some people use "Liquid Paper" in a matching shade to the paper. I do not like to use it this way if I don't have to, as it never quite matches, and if you rub over it, it will turn shiny. There are times when "Liquid Paper" is very useful, but this is not one of them.

Another approach is to use ink eradicator. The old ones were made with potassium permanganate which, although it was hard on the paper, worked. If you use potassium permanganate, then be very careful to apply it very sparingly, and put a piece of waxed paper behind the page you are working on. Let the page dry out completely before touching the area at all. Other chemicals that have been used for this purpose are oxalic acid and Chloramine T 2%. I do not like chemicals very much and don't use them; if you are really interested in them, read Cockerell (see "FURTHER READING").

I have tried using other brands of ink eradicators, at least to test them out. There is a "one-step" kind that contains sodium hypochlorite. It left the paper whiter than the surrounding area and I did not like the results. There is also a "two-step" kind that smells as though it has the same sort of chemicals. The manufacturers claim the second step "refinishes" the paper. I tried this one, too, and still was not too happy with the results, but I will admit that it was a lot better than the "one-step". If you use anything like this, remember to use it very sparingly until you see what it does. Put a piece of waxed paper behind the page you are working on, so that you do not damage the pages underneath. Also, don't fool around with good books until you are very certain of the type results you can expect.

You will never know until you try out these approaches if they will work for you and just what they will do. That is why it is very important to use a practice book; if there are not enough examples in it to work on, then add a few in different type inks. You will find that ballpoint is very much harder to remove than regular ink, and that marking pens are just not worth the bother even to try.

Pencil Marking Inside the Book

For some reason that I have never understood, people like to underline and make notes in books, especially technical books. I always find it distracting when I read a book, as what I find to be important is not necessarily the same as the person who marked it. Needless to say, I do not mark up my books.

If the notes are in ink, then you can usually remove them by erasing. Be sure to use the same care and patience that are recommended in the section on taking out prices in pencil.

If the underlines are in pencil, then I would suggest that you use an eraser stick. This is an eraser in pencil form that you can sharpen in a pencil sharpener and usually has a brush at one end.

Be certain that you get a pink one, for pencil, and not a grey one, for ink, which would be too harsh. The pink ones work well on many coloured pencils as well as on some inks. You will have to try it very carefully on each book to see what effect it has, both on the paper and the print. Some print comes up at the slightest opportunity. Work from the spine out to the edge in small strokes. Do not go back and forth, as you will have less control and will run the risk of causing damage. Use the brush to remove any leavings; to finish up, I always blow on the page to remove anything that may be floating around.

If you come across a book with a lot of underlining, it can be very tiring and frustrating work. The tendency is to get careless and sloppy as you get tired of it. To avoid this, I would suggest that you do a few pages at a time, and then mark your place with a bit of paper and come back to the book later. Luckily, underliners also seem to get tired after a while, so you find that only a part of the book has been messed up. When you find a persistent one, you curse!!

There is, of course, nothing you can do about people who use a yellow marking pen across lines of print.

Cracked Hinges

I always like to save the repairing of cracked hinges to the last, except for the outside of the book. You usually have to leave it to dry overnight, and so you know that when you check over the repair all you have left to do is to clean up the outside of the book.

When you find one hinge cracked, you should always carefully check over the other one to make sure that it is all right. Sometimes, you will find that it is wobbly but not cracked. Then you should look under "Hinges Loose But Not Cracked" in the chapter on PROBLEMS.

The first thing to do is get your tools assembled so you do not have to hunt for them at the wrong moment. You will need a piece of waxed paper folded to fit the length of the book plus a couple of inches; if you are working with a large book, you may have to fold it diagonally so it will fit. You will also need adhesive (cornflour paste is not strong enough), a small stiff brush, your blunt knife, and some sort of weights (other books, a book press, or something).

Next you should inspect the area that is cracked and make certain that it is clean. If there is a series of small cracks, it might be better to open them up so that the adhesive gets in. If you have an applicator bottle for your adhesive, lay a thin line of adhesive all the way down the crack from the top of the book right down to the bottom. You want to get enough adhesive in so that you will not only glue the paper together but will also strengthen the book, but you don't want so much that it bleeds out and becomes messy. If you do not have an applicator bottle, then use a small stiff brush, making sure it gets well into the cracked areas. Even if you have used an applicator bottle, you might want to go over it with the brush just to make certain that it is well into the crack.

Now take your blunt knife and, using the flat of it, press the edges of the paper together so they will seal and at the same time take off any excess adhesive. If you have the type of crack where there is a flap of paper left on one side, then run the knife under it and push it over to where it should be; the adhesive should help keep it down, as by now it will have become sticky. (See illustration, fig. 4.)

Put the waxed paper fold right into the fold of the hinge so that if any of the adhesive comes out under pressure it will go onto the waxed paper and not cause anything in the book to stick together. Close the book and press down on the outside of the cover all along the area that you have glued. Use the weight of your body and make sure it is well pressed. I like to open the book up at this point and make sure that it has all come together the way it should. If necessary, wipe off the excess adhesive that has leaked out with your knife; then fold the waxed paper inside out and put it back in.

Place the book in the book press or weight it down with a lot of other books (telephone books are good for this) and leave it overnight to dry.

At this point, before you forget, wash your brush out with soap and water, and dry it off. Also make sure that your blunt knife is clean.

When the repair is thoroughly dry, after about twelve hours, remove the waxed paper and test the hinge for flexibility.

Oftentimes, you will find that there are also cracks internally, within the bulk of the book. These are essentially the same as when the hinges crack, and are treated in the same way. The cracking is usually cleaner and simpler (you don't find small cracks or flaps of paper that you have to match up). Be careful that you do not put too much adhesive in repairs on internal cracks. Try not to let the adhesive creep up the pages, as it will make them stick together. Do not force the sheet of folded waxed paper down in the crack, or you will find that it will not come out well when the repair is dry, and will leave bits of waxed paper in the book: you have to get it in far enough to prevent the pages from sticking together, but not so far that it gets embedded in the repair. Sometimes the crack will happen at a section break (or signature) and the adhesive will creep out at the other side of the section; you will have to put a piece of folded waxed paper at this point as well.

Top Edge Dusty

The top edges of most books get dusty, and some even get quite dirty. You want to hold the book quite firmly with one hand wrapped around the top of the spine, fingers pointing toward the fore-edge. Now exert pressure with your fingers so that the book stays tightly closed. The first thing I do is blow along the top edge of the book from the spine toward the fore-edge. If it is still dusty,

I use a dusting brush or a feather duster. You could also vacuum the top edge with the brush attachment if you have one, observing the same instructions about holding the book tightly closed and working from the spine to the fore-edge.

If the edges are too dirty to respond to any of these treatments, then you can try harsher methods. The first might be to go over it lightly with a suede brush; be gentle about it and do not force the dirt down into the book. When you use a suede brush, you have to hold the book even more tightly closed than you would otherwise. The next step would be to try using a pencil rubber, carefully working in one direction, from the spine to the fore-edge. Keep your strokes short, and keep the book tightly closed.

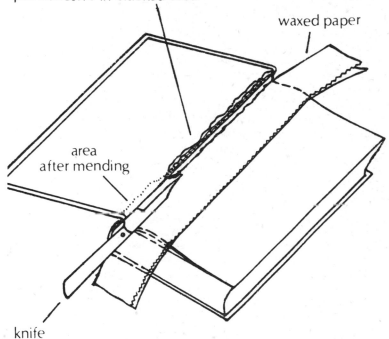

put adhesive in cracked area

waxed paper

area
after mending

knife

Cracked Hinge   **figure 4**

The edges of some books are stained and obviously these must be handled more carefully so that you do not take the colour off. Also, many older books have gilt edges and must be handled with care. The most you can do with books having gilt edges is to dust or vacuum them, or, if you are very careful about it, you can try cleaning them with soft white bread.

You may not be aware of it, but there are also books that have scenes painted on their fore-edge. These don't show when the book is closed, and are seen only when the pages are fanned out slightly. These books are usually very old and valuable, and are seen in collections of rare books.

Cover Dull and Faded

The first thing to do is to dust the cover off. If there are a lot of obvious dirty marks, you could try an eraser on them. I use a wide pencil rubber in broad strokes in one direction from the spine out to the edge. Often you will find that this will lighten the cover up so much that you will have to go over the whole thing in order to blend it evently. Erasers can also be used on paper-covered boards, but you have to be very careful that you do not damage the print. White bread is often given as a method of removing dirt; this works especially well on white covers.

Please do not even consider washing the covers of books for any reason. It may clean them up, but it also takes the sizing out of the cloth and leaves them dull and ugly looking. Not only that, but it can also get down into the boards and cause mildew, or get down into the pages and cause even more problems. There are some books that have special "washable covers"; these are primarily children's books or cook books. These usually have a plastic coating on them, but if there are cracks in the coating then you are in trouble. I prefer to use a cleaning solvent applied with a soft rag even to those covers that are supposed to be washable.

If you have stains on the covers, then you should read the chapter on PROBLEMS under headings such as "Grease", "Stains (General)" or "Cup Rings and Glass Rings". The major thing is to identify the type of stain and proceed from there. In general, I would say that most stains that are already set will not come out very easily, if at all, and it is just best to live with them.

If you have a rough cloth binding, you might try an eraser, but I find that a light treatment with the suede brush works much better.

Many times you will find discolouring and fading. This can be anything from sun-faded streaks and discoloured spines (also usually due to sun exposure) to light edges and corners of the cover due to wear.

The smaller areas due to wear are the easiest to deal with. I usually use Synchromatic Transparent Water Colour (from an art store). I have a big set of fourteen bottles which gives me a lot of possibilities, but smaller sets are available. If you do not feel that you want to invest in something like this, then you could try using a set of water-based felt-tipped pens that are primarily for artwork. Water colour dyes can be mixed to give you the colour you need. They can be put on with a cotton swab, but I find this usually gives too intense a colour. I prefer to use a clean soft rag and work the colour in; usually, the more you rub and work with it, the better it blends. This is especially true with the larger areas. If you are using the felt-tipped pens, you might try to dot the area first, and then use a very slightly damp rag to go over it and blend it in. The object is to blend the area into the colour of the rest of the cover, not to make a lot of dark spots where you had light spots before.

At times, you will find that the cloth is frayed at the corners and it should be glued down (see chapter on PROBLEMS under "Tears in Covers"). At other times, you will find that the corners are so worn there is not enough material to glue down and the best you can do is trim off the loose threads with a pair of sharp scissors.

When you get into larger areas of fade, then the problem multiplies for you. Faded spines are not too bad. You must be careful to get the colour on evenly and water colour dye is best for that, especially if you put it on a cloth and then rub it onto the book. Rather than dampen the rag with water to blend the colour, I often use saliva, which seems to work very well without getting the area too wet. Streaks and fading on the front or back cover require more work and patience. I usually go over the lightened parts first trying to match them up to the darker parts; then I go over the whole cover trying to blend it all together. I have not always had great successes with these large areas, but over a period of time, I find that if I stay with it and don't give up, it will finally blend. As with any other book you work on, you must be very careful in your approach and have a lot of patience when working with dyes. I would be very shy of using them on very expensive books even though I notice that they are talked about in books on conservation and restoration, so I doubt that they would hurt the book.

After you have done all you can in the way of erasing, brushing, cleaning, and dyeing the cover, then you should consider using a wax on it. A wax all by itself will take off the dust, brighten up the colour, and make it look a lot fresher, and, best of all, protect the book.

I used to have a wax that I got from a bindery for leather books. I had a rag that was permeated with it, and somehow I discovered that even though the wax was not recommended for use on cloth-bound books, I could really achieve a good effect by using this rag to go over my covers, and I still use it for some books. Mostly now I use a product called Renaissance Micro-Crystalline Wax. This was developed for the British Museum; it is used on all sorts of things, including paper and over artists' drawings. I apply it with a clean rag and, after a couple of minutes, buff it a little. I use it on regular cloth bindings, paper on boards, paperbacks, leather bindings, etc.; I do not use it on paperbacks with a dull finish or on rough cloth bindings, as they don't need the sheen. The instructions say to use a very small amount, and that seems to work best, so although a tin of it is rather expensive it lasts for a long time.

I feel I should point out that it says in the instructions that this product will help clean, as well. I have tried to use it for that, and do not have any luck with it in that way. It works best for me if I make sure that the cover is clean first.

Summary

Let's review some of the more important aspects of working on books:

The very first thing you need to do when you pick up a book to clean is to identify the problems. Look over it well and put slips of paper in the pages where you have problems.

The next thing is to tackle the problems from the inside of the book outward to the cover (except in the case of leather-bound books, where you treat the cover first), and from the simple to the more complex jobs, leaving anything like gluing to the last so it can stand overnight.

With each job or problem you tackle, you will have to make a decision first as to whether or not you want to do anything about it, or indeed if you can do anything about it, or are you just going to leave it alone. This will be based on your experience and the quality of the book involved. Then you will still have to approach it on an experimental basis and handle each problem carefully and with patience. It is always wise to try to remove anything in a small area and very lightly, to see if it will work well for you. Remember there is no one set way to tackle most of the problems you encounter in cleaning and repairing books. There is usually a number of options and what you decide to do is a question of both your judgement and the skills you have developed.

Do not try new methods, products, or techniques that you are not sure of on good books. In fact, the better the book is, the less you should attempt to do to it. If there are really problems with a good book, then it might be a good idea to get some professional help. One of the solutions to dealing with a really valuable old book that is falling apart is not even to rebind it, but instead to build a box for it, covered in buckram and labelled. The old cover is taken off the book, if it hasn't already come off, and put into a compartment which is built into the box under where the book lies. In this way, the book is protected and the original cover is preserved for record.

Another possible way of dealing with a book that you do not feel you are ready for is to wrap it in a brown paper bag and write the title on the outside, putting it aside until you are more competent. Some people use plastic bags, but I feel that, although plastic may seal problems out, it can also seal other problems in, especially if there is any chance of a moisture or mildew problem already in the book. Do not put rubber bands around a book in an attempt to keep its covers on it. Rubber bands leave very bad marks that are really impossible to get rid of later. Then you can practice on "practice books" or books that are not so valuable, and when you feel ready to tackle the books you have put away, you can come back to them.

The best rule of thumb I can give you is, "When in doubt, don't do it."

You should now be ready to try some of the solutions to other problems you have with your books. The problems are listed in alphabetical order in the chapter that follows.

PROBLEMS AND HOW TO DEAL WITH THEM

Please note: The suggestions given in this section should not be attempted until you have tried the operations described in the chapter on TECHNIQUES. There will probably be many you will not want to use. When possible, I have tried to give a number of solutions to any one problem, so that you can make a choice depending on the skills you have developed and the actual book you are working with. Each book must be looked upon as a case all by itself. One very possible solution always is to decide not to try to do anything about the problem at all.

Book Plates, etc.

One of the easiest solutions to a book plate problem is to sand out the person's name and put your own in. This can usually be done whether the name is written in ink or has been printed on. Another easy solution is to blank out the name with "Liquid Paper". A third solution is to put your book plate over the one that is already there.

There are times when you might want to remove the book plate altogether; I find that this is especially true with school presentation plates, as they are larger than book plates and cannot be covered over. Removing plates can be a real problem because it requires a lot of patience. The least satisfactory way to do this is to use a slightly damp (not wet) sponge, put it right on the plate, leave it there for 20 minutes or so, and hope that it has loosened the plate enough so that it will come right off. What you really want is to be able to float the plate off; once you come to an area where it is not completely loosened, you can get into trouble. Usually what happens is that some of the paper starts to come off, as well, and this usually ends up meaning that you will have to replace the flyleaves.

There are a couple of products that I have found are better ways to remove plates: (see TOOLS AND SUPPLIES for details). With either, you have to cover the entire area of the plate and leave it until you can get the blade of a blunt knife under the edge to lift the plate off. If you get any resistance, then it is best to stop and apply more to the area that is sticking, wait a bit, and try again. If you are working on the free flyleaf, you might want to put some of the solution on the back of the page, behind the plate, to help loosen it.

Even with all this, and presuming that you get the plate off well, you might not like the look of the page and may want to put a new book plate over the area.

Candle Wax

Sometimes you will find candle wax on the covers of books. The first thing to do is to try to take the excess wax off with your blunt knife or your fingernail. Usually, if you gently scrape a little with your fingernail, you can get a bit more off without hurting anything. You might also go over it lightly with a suede brush to help loosen the wax. Then I would go at it with cleaning fluid to see if I could get the rest off.

Chewing Gum

Uggh!! It does happen, unfortunately.

On the cover — (especially shiny cloth covers). Wrap the book in plastic and tape it shut, then put the book in the freezer for a couple of hours until the gum is rock hard. Then try to lift it off with a blunt knife, and clean off the residue with cleaning fluid. Be very careful with this.

On paper. If it is between the pages and they are stuck together, then carefully try to slice through the gum itself with a sharp knife in order to separate the pages. Let the gum dry out. You can aid this by putting an ice cube wrapped in plastic (securely, so it won't leak) on top of the gum. After it is hard, you can very carefully try to slice under it to remove it, or try to lift it off. You could also try to loosen it with cleaning fluid, first. If the gum has come in contact with a printed area, I would definitely try the cleaning fluid, as lifting the gum off would probably take the print with it. Above all, be very careful.

Clipped Flyleaves

Either leave it alone or, if you have managed to master the technique of replacing the flyleaves, then this is your answer (see chapter on REPLACING FLYLEAVES). There is also a way to replace an area by building up layers of rice paper, but this works better if the edge of the paper is ragged, which allows it to blend better. This is done in the manner described in "Holes in the Pages", except that when you have finished putting several layers on, you have to trim the edges to match the other pages of the book.

Coloured Paper

Some books have coloured paper, usually flyleaves (endpapers). If the colour is all the way through the page, you can erase and even do light sanding. If the colour is only on as a coating, even a light erasure will cause the colour to come off. Be very careful and test lightly, first. You will also find that many older books have very dark, dull flyleaves where the colour almost looks like a coating of clay. These are impossible to work on, as almost anything will cause them to go shiny. The same cautions apply to flyleaves that have printing on them: be very careful and test first.

Cover Fade

Badly faded covers can be gone over with water-colour dye, but it must be used carefully (see chapter on TECHNIQUES). Otherwise, a good cleaning and a coat of wax will help.

Cover Spots and Stripes

Essentially, I find that most cover stains are there to stay. It is not wise to attempt to use chemicals on covers, as you run the risk of disrupting the colour and finish of the cover.

You might want to try any of the following to see if it will help:
erasing
working at it with your fingernail or a blunt knife
working at it with a suede brush (carefully)
rubbing it with cleaning fluid
waxing the cover
Above all, DON'T EVER WASH THE COVER!!

Small worn spots can be blended in with a coloured felt-tipped pen or with water-colour dyes, as described in the chapter on TECHNIQUES.

You might also find helpful information in the section on "Cup Rings and Glass Rings" in this chapter.

Covers Detached

Basically, the book needs to be rebound. If you do not feel that it is worth it, and it is a book that you just want to keep and not handle too much, then you might consider repairing it along the lines given in "Cracked Hinges" in the chapter on TECHNIQUES, or you might put in new flyleaves. None of these methods will hold up in the long run, and if you have a lot of books with this problem, you might consider taking a bookbinding course and working on them yourself.

Covers Dull

Usually, a good brushing and waxing will help brighten them up. See the chapter on TECHNIQUES for more information.

Crayon

Apply a thick coat of rubber cement and let it dry. You can then work the rubber cement, rubbing it until it forms a ball. This should take much of the crayon up. If there is a lot left, then you will have to give it another coat of rubber cement. When you get it down to where there is just a faint discolouration, then you can usually handle this by erasing or sanding lightly. Do not try to remove crayon that is over print by this method, as it will probably lift off the print.

Cup Rings and Glass Rings

Needless to say, you should not put glasses or cups down on books, even if they are dry and cold; and I will bet you have seen other people do it, even if you have not done it yourself. The ring that you get has to be treated in terms of what caused it. Some of the things you can try are:

Tea or Coffee: cleaning fluid, or potassium permanganate, carefully, as it might also take the colour out of the cover. It works best on paper; use sparingly, with a blotter or waxed paper under the page you work on. Let it dry thoroughly.

Wine: if red wine, apply white wine with an eye dropper, then cleaning fluid; if white wine, just use cleaning fluid.

If you are interested in the use of chemicals, then you should read Cockerell (see FURTHER READING), as I have a very limited experience with them. In general, I use cleaning fluid, an eraser, and a good coat of wax, which will often lessen if not get rid of the ring.

Dealers' Name Stickers

Some booksellers use a small gummed sticker on the inside front or back cover; these can usually be lifted off with your blunt knife. If there is a residue, then cleaning fluid or a light sanding will usually take care of it. If they do not come off easily (people's return address stickers, for example), either try cleaning fluid first, or simply sand the name off the sticker. The more modern ones which have a sticky backing should be handled the same as Price Stickers, and you should see that section.

Dirt on Pages

Erase — see discussion in chapter on TECHNIQUES. Other things you can use are white bread, or a cleaning pad. Go over the area with the same care that you would with erasing.

Dirty Edges

This is discussed in detail in the chapter on TECHNIQUES under "Top Edge Dusty". The only thing I might add is that you can also use white bread in much the same way as you would use an eraser to try to remove the dirt. Also, you might want to see the section "Edges — Writing or Rubber Stamp."

Dust Jackets

Dust jackets, or dust wrappers, are primarily there to help keep the covers of the book clean. There comes a time when you must decide if a very shabby dust jacket is really serving this purpose or whether you should take it off. It is important to point out that some first editions are more valuable with their dust jackets on, but this presumes that the dust jackets are in good condition. If the dust jacket has a few tears and you think it worth saving, then I would take it off the book, turn it inside out, and tape the tears together with transparent tape. Even better would be to use rice paper and cornflour paste which is discussed under "Adhesives" in the chapter on TOOLS AND SUPPLIES. In this case, I would apply the rice paper to the back of the dust jacket only, cover it with waxed paper, and put a weight on it to dry. In any of these operations, it is important that you make certain the edges of the tear are carefully lined up, so that it looks good when you have finished.

Some dust jackets have a glossy coating and can be cleaned up with a little cleaning fluid on a soft rag. The uncoated types often respond to a careful erasing or something like a cleaning pad or white bread. If you find bits of food or other things hardened on them, try to remove them with your fingernail or your blunt knife. Removal of prices is discussed under "Price on Dust Jacket". Also, I would like to point out that if you leave a really ragged dust jacket on a book and then it is exposed to too much light, you will have a streaky faded cover after a period of time.

Dusty Covers

This is covered in detail in the chapter on TECHNIQUES. If you are working with a rough cloth cover, you might try going over it with masking tape looped around your fingers, much as you would when lifting lint off clothing. Otherwise, a suede brush used gently works quite well. You will find leather bindings discussed in the section on "Leather Bindings."

Edges — Writing or Rubber Stamp

This is definitely a case where you have to determine if you are going to tackle the problem or not. There is no sure way to remove writing or rubber stamps from the edges. The first thing to do is to try a suede brush, and the next to try an eraser; make sure in each case that you hold the book very tightly closed and work from the spine out to the fore-edge, if you are working on the top or bottom edge. Sometimes sand-paper, used very carefully, will work; but it usually doesn't get it all off, and it will leave the area you are working on lighter than the rest, which does not look too good. As a last resort, and if you are really determined to blot out whatever is there, you might use a matching shade of Liquid Paper.

In any case, I would urge you to exercise great care and really determine if the writing, etc., *must* be done away with. It is never an easy job, and the results are not always very satisfactory.

Flowers and Leaves Pressed In

In the first place, don't do it. If you really feel that you must press flowers and things in books, you should do it between two pieces of waxed paper or blotting paper. If you find flowers and leaves in a book, remove them; if they have left stains, see "Stains, General".

Folded Down Corners

The first thing to do is carefully straighten them out to where they should be. If you have a book press, you should put the book in for a few hours; if not, you should weight the book down. If the paper has started to crack at these folds, you could reinforce the area with rice paper. See the section on "Holes in Pages" for the basic techniques of how to handle this.

Foxing

As far as I know, there is basically nothing you can do about this condition. I have always been told it is due to an iron problem in the paper. Recently, I read in Cockerell a recommendation of Chloramine T 2% solution for this, but I have had very little experience with chemicals and shy away from using many of them.

Grease

Sometimes I find grease, usually greasy fingerprints, on books, both inside and out. The best way I have found to get rid of this is with cleaning fluid on a soft rag. Remember to test it out lightly first. Usually, cleaning fluid will not cause any trouble, unless you have a very unstable colour to deal with, or unstable print. If you do find any colour coming off on your rag, then be very careful that you do not take up so much that it shows.

Hinges Loose But Not Cracked

The book will feel wobbly, and if you look at it closely you will find that the part of the flyleaf that is attached to the inside cover is just starting to come away at the hinge.

Stand the book up on end and open the cover out. This will create a gap at the top. Let a small amount of adhesive dribble down between the inside cover and the flyleaf where it is coming away. Using a thin knitting needle, gently push it down this separation, carrying the adhesive down with it. Go about halfway down the length of the spine and then turn the book over and repeat the operation so that you have adhesive down the entire length of the hinge. Fold a piece of waxed paper and put it into the hinge area just as you would for repairing a cracked hinge, even though there is no adhesive exposed. This is important because there may be tiny cracks you don't see, or just the moisture in the adhesive might carry it through the paper of the flyleaf. Press along the outside of the cover, over the area where you have put the adhesive, and then make certain there is no glue coming out at the top or bottom of the hinge area; if there is, wipe it off. Put the book in a book press or under some weight and let it dry overnight.

If you find this condition in one hinge area (front or back), then carefully check the other one; you will probably need to work on it, too. The next day, remove the waxed paper and test the hinges for flexibility, etc.

Holes in the Page

If done carefully, you can usually take care of this. However, it is a repair, and will not look like the original. Using a long-fibre rice-paper, tear off a piece slightly larger than the hole. If you find it easier to cut the paper, then make it a bit larger still, and pull the edges along the cuts so that it frays. Put a piece of waxed paper behind the page you are working on. Carefully apply a thin coat of adhesive to the rice paper patch with a brush. The cornflour paste mentioned under TOOLS AND SUPPLIES works well for this, but you can also use the other adhesives mentioned. Apply the patch to cover the hole and go over it lightly with your brush to blend it into the paper. Now put a piece of waxed paper over this and turn the page over. Put a patch on the other side, as well. Replace the waxed paper and close the book; put it into the book press for several hours or, even better, overnight.

When thoroughly dry, remove the waxed paper carefully. If the patch is not strong enough, you will have to apply another layer of rice paper. Even if the rice paper goes over a printed area, it should look fairly good, and you will be able to read print through a good rice paper. Of course, if the hole is in the middle of a printed area, you are going to be minus that amount of text. It is possible to find a good copy of the book and photocopy the missing area (for both sides of the page), fit the copies to the hole, and put a rice paper patch over the top.

Ink Underlining

Basically, there is not much you can do about this. If you try to remove the ink, you will probably remove the print, as well. You can try a pencil stick eraser, very carefully, but it is very tricky; see chapter on TECHNIQUES. I only use pink pencil stick erasers, as the grey ones will take the print up. If the underlining goes out into the margin, you might want to try to remove this part of it. One of the ways you could try is a very light stroke with sandpaper.

Ink Marks and Names

See chapter on TECHNIQUES for a full discussion.

Insect Stains

Try to remove any residue with your fingernail or blunt knife. Try erasing, being especially careful if it is over a printed area. If it is not over a printed area, you might even try a light sanding to remove the stain. In the way of chemicals, the first thing I would try is an application of cleaning fluid. Other things you could try would be equal parts of peroxide and alcohol, or Chloramine 2% solution (see section on "Stains General").

Leather Bindings

The first thing to remember when you are working on a book with a full or partial leather binding is that you should treat the cover before you tackle the rest of the book. Whatever else you have to do to the book you would do in the same manner as for other books, and then when you are all finished, it is always a good idea to go back over the covers once again. I usually apply a preservative such as potassium lactate if the covers look at all dry. After that is dry, I use one of the many leather waxes available. I have mentioned a couple of them in the chapter on TOOLS AND SUPPLIES, and mentioned others under "Suppliers".

I understand that saddle soap can be used to clean up bindings that are especially dirty, but I would caution you, if you do use it, that you be very careful with the amount of water you use and also be very careful to keep the moisture away from the inside of the book.

If you find problems with mould, you can try going over the cover with a soft rag that has been dampened with ammonia before you do anything else.

Older leather-bound books develop a problem called "red rot", where the leather simply crumbles away. I would suggest if you have this problem, or if you have a lot of leather-bound books, that you read Middleton's *Restoration of Leather Bindings.*

Suede bindings are not handled in the same way. See section on "Suede Bindings".

Library Numbers on Spine

What you can do about this depends in large part on how they were put there in the first place. If it is with white ink, then you can usually scrape it off with your fingernail or your blunt knife. Going over the area lightly with a suede brush will also help lift some of it off. Then you can go over the area with wax. If the area is badly discoloured, you might consider using water-colour dye on it before waxing. The use of these dyes is covered in the chapter on TECHNIQUES.

Many libraries use a shellac, or something like it, over their numbers. Some of these will scrape off with the blunt knife, and you should consider yourself lucky if they do; but many of the others seem not to come off, whatever you do. I have had some luck with cleaning fluid, and certainly it won't hurt to try. You could also try methyl, or wood, alcohol, which will soften certain older types of varnish and shellac. If you come up against a stubborn one, it is probably best just to leave it on. Certainly you should not use brute force or anything really harsh, as it might hurt the book.

Marking Pens

Sometimes you run across marking pens used for people's names, prices, scribbles, or you might find a yellow one used to give over "important" passages, in places of underlining. There is nothing that will take it out, as far as I know, because it soaks into, and sometimes through, the paper, but some of it can be dealt with when necessary.

If you need to get rid of prices, the most effective way is to use a Liquid Paper in a shade that comes close to the paper. If necessary, you might have to apply it to both sides of the paper, as some of that stuff bleeds through. It will probably not look like the original paper, but it will look better than it did before.

There are times when you can put a bookplate over a name very effectively. This works especially well if the name is on the inside cover; if it is on the free flyleaf, you will often find you have to put a coat of Liquid Paper on the other side after using a bookplate, as it still shows through.

Sanding this type of marking is usually a waste of time, as you have to remove too much of the paper for the sanding to work.

An old secretarial trick of the trade is to use a pump-type hair spray to remove marking pen ink from both the hands and the clothes. It's certainly worth trying, especially if there is an area where a little experimentation won't damage the book. Or try it on a practice book.

Mildew

I always dread it when I run into mildew. If it is among my own books, it means that I have a problem in the room; dealing with the book is secondary to finding out where the damp is coming in. This aspect is discussed in the chapter on MAINTAINING YOUR LIBRARY. If you find mildew on a book coming in, then you should deal with it right away, so that it does not spread.

Brush the mildew off the book. If the book is damp, then dry it, using the methods outlined in the section on "Wet Books". After the book is thoroughly dry, there are a number of things you can try in order to deal with the mildew:

Hydrogen peroxide, carefully applied to the area with an eyedropper;
Lemon juice, applied with an eyedropper, and the book placed in the sun for a short time only, as you don't want to remove the cover colour;
Denatured alcohol, applied with a soft rag or cotton wash;
Thymol in a solution of alcohol.
Be careful with all of these solutions that you blot up any excess.

If the mildew has got to the pages, then you can sprinkle diatomaceous earth between the pages, leave it for several days to dry, and brush or vacuum it out.

If you find that you have to deal with a number of books with a mildew problem, I definitely suggest that you read Cockerell, Horton or one of the other books on conservation.

Mildew often leaves spots on a cover after you have got rid of it. Or more often you will find a book that had mildew and what you have to deal with is the spots that are left. As these are usually lighter than the cover colour, they can be blended in with water-colour dyes, which you can read about in the chapter on TECH-NIQUES. If they are dark spots, then you might try lemon juice or a weak solution of peroxide; in both cases, be very careful and apply small amounts with an eyedropper, wiping the solution off before the action goes too far. After you have dealt with the spot, apply a coat of Renaissance Wax or some other good wax for protection.

Name on Flyleaf

To deal with this, look under the section that applies to what type of material was used, i.e., pencil, ink, marking pen, etc., to see what can be done.

Newspaper Cuttings Pasted In

It is usually a tricky job to deal with these, and if you find you are going to have any trouble I would seriously consider leaving them in. The determining factor is how well they are pasted down and what they were put in with.

If they were put in with rubber cement, then you might try applying some rubber cement thinner with a rag, in the hope that they will come right off. If they are just lightly tacked in at the corners, you might be able to lift them off with a little pressure, and if there is a residue left, try to remove it with cleaning fluid. If you meet any real resistance or you can see that they are well glued down, then it is really best to leave them alone.

It should be obvious to you by this time that I am strongly against the practice of gluing newspaper cuttings in books. If you feel that you must store them in books, then put them between two pieces of waxed paper and just lay them in. The waxed paper is there to prevent them from staining the book if they discolour, as they often do.

If you find stains of this type around newspaper cuttings in a book, you should realise that if you do succeed in removing the cutting you will still have the stain. These stains are like foxing, in that they are really impossible to get rid of. Therefore, I would think twice about trying to remove them.

Outer Spine Coming Off

Of course, the best solution to this would be to have the book rebound, but sometimes it is not the most practical solution, as the book may not be worth rebinding, or you may not have the money for it, or something.

Presuming that the rest of the spine area is in good shape, you might consider putting the outer spine back on with adhesive. You need to leave a certain amount of flexibility, so you want to apply the adhesive along the two long edges where it is actually torn, and not all over the entire piece. Press the piece back on to the book, trying to match it up as carefully as possible. If you run the flat of your blunt knife along it, it should help press it into place and force any excess adhesive out, so you can wipe it off.

The next step is to wrap a piece of waxed paper over the entire area, and then take a stretch bandage and wrap the book exactly as if it were a sprained ankle. Make the wrapping snug, but not crushingly tight. Do not use rubber bands, as they will leave bad marks that are fairly impossible to get out. I usually put another book on top of this package to prevent the wrapping from working loose, and then leave it overnight.

The next day, it should be checked for neatness and to be sure the book is flexible. If there are any threads that are loose, giving the book a frayed look, then it would be best to take them off with scissors.

If more of the spine has been pulled away, it may be necessary to make a brown-paper tube, glue this to the back of the sections and then replace the outer spine as above.

I would not suggest using cloth tape over the split, unless it is a work book or reference book that you handle a lot and use as a "work horse". The real problem with cloth tape is that it can never be satisfactorily removed later by someone who might want to repair the book another way.

Paint on Cover

Quite often, I find paint on the covers of books. Tiny flecks will usually come right up with the blunt knife; try taking any residue up with cleaning fluid. Larger amounts should be worked over with cleaning fluid and the blunt knife (be careful not to damage the cover). Do not use paint thinner or paint remover, as these will probably take the cover colour off as well. However, you can often get good results by softening the old paint with spirits of gum turpentine and then lifting it with the blunt knife. This should be tried in a small area first to test the cover for colour fastness. Often a light brushing with a suede brush will help take up light residue. Wax as usual, afterward.

Paperback Spine Pulling Away

This can be put back on in much the same way as described in "Outer Spine Coming Off", except that you can put the adhesive over the entire spine. However, it is easier and faster to use a glue stick (made for paper). It also turns out to be a lot less messy.

If the spine is just pulling away in small places, you can force some glue into the opening with your blunt knife. I dig the glue out of the glue stick. Glue stick dries quickly, and is so sticky that usually you do not have to do anything more than press the area well with your thumb.

If you have put too much glue on and it comes out, then it should be cleaned up right away, before it has a chance to dry or to get on something else.

Paperbacks

Good soft-bound books are getting so expensive that they are really worth taking care of.

Basically, they respond to many of the techniques that you would use when dealing with a hardback book, except that you have to be a lot more careful with them. The covers will often respond to being erased, and glossy covers can be gone over with a small amount of cleaning fluid on a clean rag.

I have recently read an interesting book on how to clothbind a paperback book, which I have listed for further reading. If you had anything that was valuable, however, I would suggest making a box for it, in order to preserve it in its original form.

Paperback — Section Pulling Out

This seems to happen a lot, especially on some of the books that are bound cheaply by the so-called 'perfect binding' method. If the section is not really out, but just cracked at the hinge, then you would proceed just as you would for a hardbound book. This is discussed in the chapter on TECHNIQUES at the end of the section on "Cracked Hinges".

If the section is all the way out, then it needs to be glued back in. Apply the adhesive to the back of the section with a brush and make certain that it is well spread out and not too thick. Position it carefully back into the space where it belongs and place a piece of folded waxed paper on both sides of it, well back toward the spine but not too far back to become stuck in the crack between the pages. You must see that it is well lined up by pressing it into place with your fingers, and make certain that the back of the spine is well pressed onto it so that there is a positive contact. Any excess adhesive is forced out the top and bottom of the spine, where it can be wiped off.

Put the book in the press or under weights overnight. When it is thoroughly dry, remove the waxed paper and test it for flexibility. The danger points are that you either put too much adhesive on it in the beginning, or that you do not line it up carefully and so cause it to stick out beyond the rest of the pages.

If the section has pulled out in a messy fashion and there are loose pages, then I would put it all together, line it up very carefully, and a glue a piece of rice paper covering the entire back and about half an inch of the front and back pages of the section. If you can get it back together as a secure and tight section, you have a better chance of getting it back into the book in the right manner and so that it will hold well. Don't worry if the rice paper comes up over some of the print on the front and back pages; you should be able to read through it without any problem. Once you have this together, you glue it back into the book as outlined above.

This method can also be used with sewn-bindings. Where a signature (section) is pulling out, usually partially and you do not have the ability to re-sew it; nor is the book worth taking to a binder. Just gluing it back is a solution. It may not be the best solution, but it is better than ignoring it on a book that you want to be serviceable but is not really worth much.

Paper Clips

Don't use paper clips in books. When you find them in books, take them out right away. Even if they have not rusted, they will leave an impression in the paper, and might even affect a number of pages.

If the impression is not too old, it might just relax out, especially if you weight the book down, closed, overnight. If necessary, you can help it by dampening the paper very slightly and then drying it under weight, having put a piece of waxed paper on either side of the page.

If the paper clip has left rust stains (and this seems to happen a lot), you should read the section entitled "Rust Stains".

Paper Separating

This occurs on the edges of paperback covers; sometimes a layer of paper will lift up on a dust jacket, etc. I find that the best thing to use is glue stick, as it is easy to use and dries quickly. If the area you are dealing with is not too accessible, then dig the glue out of the stick with your blunt knife and force it into the separated area that way.

Pencil Underlinings

Use a pencil eraser stick carefully to try to get them out (see chapter on TECHNIQUES.) Be sure the eraser is for pencils and not an ink eraser.

Periodicals

Many people collect old periodicals. They were not originally made to last very long, and easily show signs of wear. Most of the repairs that you can make on them are the same as you would use for a book or a paperback. Above all, you must be careful about how you handle and store them, so that they do not get progressively worse.

Some of the things you might want to consider are:

straightening out any bent page corners;
carefully erasing dirt off covers or pages;
repairing any cracked or torn pages with rice paper;
repairing any torn hinges with rice paper;
weighting them down flat, either in a book press or under telephone books, for several days.

If you are not familiar with using rice paper, then you should read the sections called "Holes in the Page" and "Tears in Pages".

Storage of periodicals is important; they do better if they are laid down flat, rather than being stored standing on edge. Some people wrap them, usually in groups, in plastic wrap, which makes them easier to handle. This is all right if you have no moisture in the periodicals; it will seal the moisture out and make them easier to handle without fear of further wear. The wrap can be removed easily enough when you want to use them. Other options are to build storage boxes for them, or to have them bound in groups or series. Maybe a bookbinding course would make it possible for you to bind them yourself.

Plates Loose

In this case, "plates" means full-page illustrations. The way in which some books are bound allows them to separate and come out, whereas the printed text pages will not do that. They can be carefully tipped back in with a narrow strip of rice paper.

Cut a piece of rice paper just barely short of the length of the plate and about an inch wide. Fold it in half lengthwise. Then you want to glue half of it onto the spine edge of the plate and the other half will be glued onto the preceding page, with the fold going down into the spine crack. It is almost always necessary to trim about a quarter of an inch off the plate on the spine side so that when you have it all glued in place the fore-edge will line up with the rest of the pages.

You can also often put them directly back in with adhesive and protected with folded waxed paper on each side until they are dry. This is the same technique discussed under "Paperback — Section Pulling Out", except you are working with a single page instead of a whole section. You should watch that you do not put too much adhesive on and that you line the plate up carefully with the rest of the pages so that it does not stick out when you are through. That is probably the hardest thing to do.

Whether you glue it back directly or use rice paper, it is a job that requires a lot of patience and accuracy. I would not attempt it until you have a lot of experience and feel confident about being able to handle it.

Price on Dust Jacket

Usually, this is in a corner and it can easily be cut off with a pair of scissors. Other options are to cover it up with Liquid Paper or sand it off with sandpaper. Sometimes it is in an inconvenient place on the dust jacket where you would not want to cut it out, so one of these other options will work better for you.

Price Stickers

I am finding a lot of sticky price stickers, these days. In fact, I bought a book at a charity sale some time ago that had one on the cover, and made several mistakes about it. First, I should have noticed that the cover was paper over boards, and not cloth. Second, when I went to take the sticker off, I should have tried cleaning fluid on it first to see if it would lift, rather than trying to remove it with just a blunt knife and taking part of the cover with the label. Needless to say, I was not very happy about it. Considering the prices charged for books these days, it was an all round bad deal.

Now I apply a little cleaning fluid to all price stickers first, no matter where they are. Then I ease a corner up with my blunt knife. I usually take hold of this corner with my fingers and pull slowly, using the knife in the other hand to hold down the paper underneath so that it does not come up, too. Then, after I am finished, I go over the area again with a little cleaning fluid to take up any of the sticky stuff that may still be there. I leave the book to dry thoroughly.

Printed and Decorated Flyleaves

Some books, especially older ones, have decorated flyleaves which can be anything from a printed design or marbled paper to having the illustrations on the flyleaves. You have to take the same precautions that I have noted about coloured paper. It is very difficult to remove anything from flyleaves of this type, as even erasing can cause the design to come off. If you do want to try to erase, you should approach it very carefully and try out a small area first. If there is any lightening of the design, you should stop. I would even be careful when using cleaning fluid, especially if the flyleaves are hand marbled.

Protecting the Corners of Covers

There are times when you want to protect the corners of your books, especially if you are sending a valuable book through the post. The fancy way to do this is with a piece of soft metal covered with paper. See illustration fig. 5.

A. Place a piece of soft metal 2" wide by 1" on a piece of paper $2\frac{1}{2}$ inches square.
B. Bend the metal at the dotted lines and fold the upper two corners to the centre, but not all the way down flat.
C. Shows what it looks like. You just slip it over the corner.

You can obtain these ready made, too.

The way to make these without the soft metal is to take two pieces of brown sticky wrapping tape each $2\frac{1}{2}$ inches square, wet

56

Folding a Corner Protector
figure 5

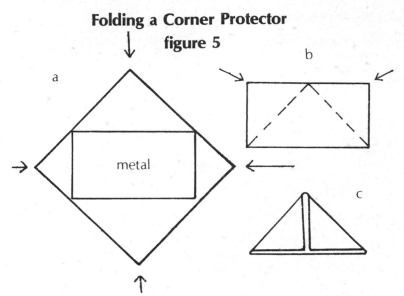

them and stick them together with the sticky sides together. Then fold them as above and let them dry thoroughly before using them.

Rubber Cement

Rubber cement has its uses, but it is really not strong enough to use when repairing books. What I use it for is removing crayon and grease pencil, which is explained in the section titled "Crayon". If you find that other people have used rubber cement in a book, it is usually very easy to remove, as you can rub it with your finger and it will roll up into a ball and come off. Sometimes when it is under something you may want to use a little rubber cement thinner on it first.

You should re-work any repairs that have been made with rubber cement. I found a book the other day in which someone had tried to repair a cracked hinge with rubber cement, and of course it was not holding. I rubbed off what I could without hurting the book, and took the rest off with rubber cement thinner before proceeding to repair the hinge in the proper manner.

Rubber Stamp Marks

The only good thing you can say for rubber stamps is that they usually do not leave an impression in the paper. Of course, how far the ink penetrates into the paper depends upon the paper itself and how much ink was on the stamp at the time.

Erasing will usually not do much about these marks. If you are careful, you can try to lift them off with a light sanding. If you decide to try this, make sure you read about the problems involved in the chapter on TECHNIQUES. Another possibility is using Liquid Paper in a matching shade, but as I have said before this usually shows somewhat after you have finished.

Rust Stains

These are usually caused by staples or paper clips. There are several approaches to this problem, and none of them is a sure thing. You can try a light sanding to see if that will lift it. You can try Liquid Paper in a shade matching the paper, but it will probably show. You can try hydrogen peroxide applied with an eye dropper or a glass rod, very carefully; make sure you blot up the excess. Potassium permanganate will also remove rust, but it is very tricky to use and you have to be very, very careful with it.

Sections Coming Out

When the sections start coming out of a hardbound book, it is time for rebinding. If you feel that the book is not worth being rebound and you just want to keep it together to use as a work book, or what is called a "reading copy", then you could review the section on "Cracked Hinges" in the chapter on TECHNIQUES, and the section on "Paperback — Section Coming Out" in this chapter.

"Scotch"-type Tape

This is really the wrong type of thing to use in books. The only time I use it is when repairing dust jackets, and then only on the underside. Apparently, some makes of Transparent Mending Tape will yellow but will not affect the paper; I am afraid I would not chance it.

Hexane is the most recommended thing for lifting tape off, and also I have had good luck with both rubber cement thinner and cleaning fluid. Apply with a clean cloth to the entire area, then try to lift a corner of the tape with a blunt knife. After you get it started, make sure that some fluid gets under the edge, and this will help you lift it off. Sometimes it helps if you apply the fluid to the other side of the page; when it soaks through, it loosens the tape. If the tape is old, you will usually have bad marks left on the paper; there is little you can do to get rid of them.

Stains — General

When dealing with stains, the first thing to do is try to determine just what caused them; sometimes what will eliminate one type of stain will set another type. The next consideration is what type of material they are on, i.e. are they on the cover or inside the book, and what is the nature of the materials used for these areas.

If the stains are on the paper and have not soaked too far into the paper, there is always the possibility of trying to erase them or giving them a light sanding. You can also try a shade of Liquid Paper that matches the paper, but the match is never perfect and it is usually apparent that you have done it.

Wine stains, either on paper or on the covers, can be dealt with as follows:

White wine can often be removed with cleaning fluid applied with a soft rag or cotton.

Red wine can often be diluted with white wine; after the colour disappears, treat it the same way as white wine.

When doing any of this, use either (or both) blotting paper or waxed paper behind the page you are working on, if you are working on the inside of the book. Also, be careful when applying the wine; you should use an eye dropper or a glass rod, apply it sparingly, and blot up any excess.

One way to get rid of stains is with chemicals and bleaching agents. I am very wary of any and all of these methods and usually do not use them. The best authority I have found is Cockerell; if you are interested in these methods, I suggest you get his book from a library and investigate further. Some of the things he talks about are citric acid, lemon juice, oxalic acid, potassium permanganate, hydrogen peroxide, and Chloramine T in a 2% solution (2 oz. Chloramine T powder to 5 pints water; the resulting solution is fairly mild). He also talks about using ultra-violet light and sunlight.

Above all, you must remember if you use any of these methods or substances that they are inherently damaging to books and must be used very sparingly and with great caution.

Suede Bindings

These are not treated the same as leather bindings. Do not use any oily or waxy preparations on them; they will lose their nap and look awful. The best thing to do is brush the covers. If there are problem spots, you can use a suede brush lightly to see if you can lift them off. You can also use masking tape with the sticky side out, wrapped around your fingers, in a lifting motion. Cleaning fluid can also be used, but carefully, so you don't leave any rings. I usually use cleaning fluid lightly over the entire cover, with an emphasis on the soiled area, to avoid rings.

Sun-Faded Covers

It is hard to blend sun fade back into the original colour of the cover, but this can be worked at with water colour dyes. See the chapter on TECHNIQUES for details on how to use them.

Tape, Cloth

Some people use a cloth tape to try to repair books, especially along the outside spine. Quite frankly, I don't like it and would not do it unless the book was a work book used for reference and was beyond repair. One of the major problems with this type of tape is that you cannot usually get it completely off, as it seems to leave a white residue. Also, you should be careful if you are trying to remove it that you do not pull part of the cover away, too. Try to soften it with Hexane or cleaning fluid, then carefully lift it off.

If you have repairs to do where you think you would like to use this type of tape, read the sections on "Outer Spine Coming Off" and "Tears in Covers", use those methods, instead.

Tears in Covers

Oftentimes, you will find small tears in cloth covers, especially along the spine area. You can usually deal with these by forcing a small amount of adhesive into the area with your blunt knife. Press the edges together with the flat of the blade or your finger, and wipe off any excess adhesive that there may be. Wrap the book in waxed paper and then with a stretch bandage, snugly and firmly, but not enough to crush the book or damage it in any way. I like to put a weight on the book or put the whole thing in the press for several hours. When it is dry, remove the bandage and waxed paper and inspect the repair. If there are any tiny threads that did not get glued, you can cut them off with a pair of scissors. Do not use rubber bands, as they leave bad dents in books.

Tears in Pages

I have heard about several methods of repairing tears in pages, but the way I like to do it is to make a patch with rice paper. It is important to use a good rice paper for repairs, one that has a long fibre, so that when you tear it, it leaves ragged fibres that will blend into the paper and not show up so much as a straight cut. You can usually find this at an artists' supply store, and one sheet should last for a very long time. Tear off a patch that will extend $\frac{1}{8}$" to $\frac{1}{4}$" on either side of the tear. Or you can cut a patch slightly bigger and then pull on the edges to fray them.

Slide the patch in between the two halves of the tear so that half the patch is on the top side of the page and half the patch is on the bottom side. This probably sounds more complicated than it is (see illustrations fig. 6). When using rice paper, you can use the flour paste formula given in TOOLS AND SUPPLIES, or any of the adhesives mentioned in that section. Then use a stiff brush to apply adhesive to the underside of the rice paper on both sides of the page. It is best to work with two pieces of waxed paper so that no matter which way you turn the page you will have waxed paper under it. You do not want to use a lot of adhesive when doing this, and if there is any excess, get it off. I like to go over the top of the patch with my brush, too, especially around the edges to blend it all in.

Close up the book, with the waxed paper in place on both sides of the page; put the book in the press or under weights, and leave it overnight. When the patch has dried, you should peel off the waxed paper very slowly and carefully. Even if the area you have worked on was printed, you should be able to read it easily through the rice paper patch.

Tears in Glossy Pages

Repairs on glossy paper are best made by applying a very small amount of adhesive to the edges of the tear with a brush, and pressing them together. The book is then closed with the page between two pieces of waxed paper, and placed under weights to dry overnight. Please read the section immediately before this one. Essentially, we are doing the same thing, except we do not use rice paper as it would be too obvious against the glossy paper.

Thin Spots on Pages

Sometimes you find these in books. It is to be hoped you have not caused them yourself by excess erasing or sanding. If you find them on the flyleaves you can always replace the flyleaf if you have developed that sort of skill (see separate chapter on this operation). Otherwise, you can apply a rice paper patch, much along the lines given in the section on "Holes in Pages". Whether or not you apply patches to both sides of the page will depend upon how much damage has been done.

Another approach, which is far less desirable, is to apply a couple of coats of Liquid Paper in a shade that matches the page, keeping a piece of waxed paper behind the page until it is thoroughly dry. As I have pointed out before, you usually do not get a perfect match with Liquid Paper.

Top of Spine Damage

Many people have a tendency to get books out of shelves by putting their finger on the top edge of the book right at the spine and pulling on the spine. Well bound books have a headband which is a piece of cord bound in at this area to help strengthen the cloth so it won't tear. Most commercially bound books nowadays do not have any reinforcement on the top of the spine, so you often find this area worn and torn.

The possibilities of putting in a headband once the damage has been done, are not very great. It is an awkward place to work in, unless you are rebinding the book.

What you can do, however, is to strengthen the area from the back. You can use buckram, especially scraps of buckram that you might have left over from making covers. You can also use drapery buckram, heavy muslin, canvas, crinoline, or nylon tulle, depending upon what you can get and what seems to work well for you.

Cut a piece of your material an inch or so long and just slightly narrower than the spine area. Insert the material behind the cloth area of the spine to see that it fits properly. You will have to open up the covers and stand the book upright to do this.

Remove the piece; if you are happy with the fit, spread a thin layer of adhesive on the material. Be careful that you do not get it on too thick: you do not want a lot of excess, as it will be hard to remove. Reinsert the material behind the cloth spine with the glued side toward the cloth so that it will stick down to it.

Put a piece of waxed paper several inches long between this repair and the spine area of the pages so that any seepage of glue will not stick. Press the area carefully to make certain that it is going to stick down well and smoothly.

At this point, I would also put a piece of waxed paper around the outside the spine, as adhesive has a way of seeping through damaged areas, and wrap the book in a stretch bandage. Wrap it securely and snugly, but not snugly enough to constrict or damage it. Put a weight on this package and leave it for several hours or even overnight.

When the area is thoroughly dry, remove the bandage and all the waxed paper, both inside and out. You should test the hinges for flexibility.

You may find that you have strengthened the spine, but it still does not look good. If there are threads sticking out, then you can snip these off with a sharp scissors. If the colour has come off the area, you can fix this with a coloured felt-tipped pen or water-colour dyes. You should see the chapter on TECHNIQUES for details on this operation.

You should also check to see that the hinges have not been weakened. If they have, then they should be repaired according to the instructions given in "Hinges Loose But Not Cracked". If they are cracked, then the instructions for repair are in the chapter on TECHNIQUES.

Vellum Bindings

I really have no experience with this type of binding except for what we did in bookbinding class. I would suggest that you read about them in Horton (see FURTHER READING), as she gives a fairly detailed discussion on how to deal with them.

Washed Covers

DON'T WASH COVERS!! It takes out the sizing and leaves the cover looking dull and awful. There are some books, especially children's books, that have a plastic coating which the publishers claim is washable. I don't even wash these; I use cleaning fluid on a soft rag, because if there are any splits in the plastic there will be trouble. If you have a cloth or paper cover that is dirty, then you should read about this in the chapter on TECHNIQUES.

If you come across a cover that has been washed, and it will be obvious right away that that is what happened, about the only thing you can do is apply Renaissance Wax, which will restore some of the lustre. Don't expect it to look like it should, because it won't.

Water

Keep it away from your books. There are times when you want a slightly damp rag to help you blend something, but that means slightly damp, not wet. I usually use saliva; it works well, and it is safer.

Water Stains

There is very little you can do about water stains, especially when they are on the pages of a book. If you have water stain on the cover of a book, you should apply some Renaissance Wax, which will help the appearance, but it will never look completely right. See sections on "Washed Covers".

Wet Books

The faster you can catch them, the better. There are a couple of approaches you can use, depending upon what materials you have available and how many books you have to deal with at the same time.

One of the best methods is to put blotting paper between the leaves of the book and weight it down. You will have to change all the blotting paper every half-hour until the leaves are dry. Another method is to stand the book up and prop it open so that the leaves are relatively free, and then use an electric hair dryer on it. You can also use an electric heater with a good fan, but don't set them too close together, and do stay with it. Don't just hope everything will be all right and leave them that way. If you have a lot of books to deal with, the best thing to do is to get them all stood up and propped open, preferably somewhere where there is a breeze, and then deal with the most valuable ones first.

The major thing to watch for in a situation where you have wet or damp books is mildew. It is difficult to get rid of, and it will thrive in damp, warm, stagnant conditions. Keep books in a place where they get a cool breeze and you lessen the chances of mildew. You should read the section on mildew anyway, as you will probably run into it sooner or later. Also, you should read the chapter on MAINTAINING YOUR LIBRARY if you are finding any evidence of dampness in your books.

Tears in Pages

figure 6

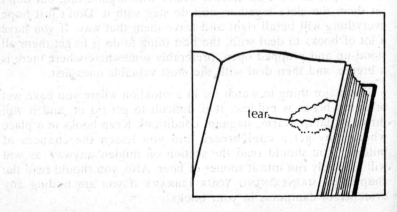

tear

REPLACING FLYLEAVES

Replacing flyleaves is, to my way of thinking, really a subject for a bookbinding class. I was reluctant to include it at all, but then when I thought about it I realized that it was really worth explaining how this is done.

Many of my attitudes towards books changed as soon as I learned how to replace flyleaves. I used to avoid books which had the free flyleaf torn out, or books where the flyleaves were cut or really messed up.

Now, instead of looking at books of this type as a problem, I just look at them as a lot of work!!!

For the sake of clarity, let me repeat the tools you will need for this operation, for you should get them together before you start:

Book press — it is really hard to do this without one.
Cutting knife — with a good, sharp blade.
Bookboard or binder's board — about 3" wide, and longer than the longest edge of the book.
Folding bone — not essential, but very helpful.
Old telephone book, or other waste paper.
Wide, short brush — for spreading adhesive.
Short, stiff oil brush — for tipping-in work.
Adhesive — in a jar you can get a brush into.
Steel ruler — must be flat.
Waxed paper.
Scissors.
Suitable paper for the flyleaves.

The first thing to do is inspect the flyleaves that have to be replaced; if they have already been torn out, remove all the loose edges and bits.

If you have to remove the flyleaf, hold the rest of the pages down with the palm of one hand, pressing down with the weight of your body, so that the book does not move around. With the other hand, slowly pull the leaf away from the bulk of the pages, back over the hinge and inside cover. It should come away smoothly and easily.

If there is a great excess of paper left on the inside cover at this point, then make sure that the surface is smooth. If necessary, go over it with sandpaper so that there are no ridges or lumps.

If you have to replace one flyleaf in a book, it is a very good idea to consider replacing the flyleaf at the opposite end of the book, too, even though it may be in perfect condition. The reason for this is so that the flyleaves at both ends of the book will be uniform and will enhance the look of the book.

The type of paper you use to make the flyleaves is very important. I use a handmade paper, because you can fold it in either direction. That is a great advantage when you are dealing with several different sizes of books and you don't want to waste a lot of expensive paper. If you do not use a handmade paper, you have to make certain that the grain is parallel to the spine of the book, i.e. it has to run from the top to the bottom, and not across, or the paper will not fold well and you must have a good sharp fold at the spine. In the long run, it is just better to invest in a good paper and not have to worry about it.

The paper I use is a handmade charcoal or watercolour paper which can be found in pads at any good artists' supply store. If you have any doubts as to whether or not it is handmade, ask the person who works in the store. Handmade paper has no grain, and you want to make certain that the paper you buy does not have a grain. Also, you want to buy a good-quality, medium-weight paper. You do not want one that is either too thin and insubstantial or so thick and heavy that it is bulky.

The paper must now be folded so that you have the two parts of the flyleaves: the part that will be glued down to the inside cover, and the free flyleaf. If you have a folding bone, it will be a lot easier; if you do not have one, then use the back of a ruler.

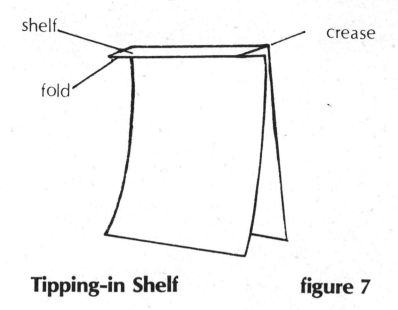

Tipping-in Shelf **figure 7**

It is essential to get a good, sharp fold. Line up the free edges so that you have two equal parts and use the bone to press down the fold, working it back and forth so that you get a crease in the paper.

If the folded sheet is a lot larger than the book, you will want to trim it at this point, so that you won't have too much paper to deal with. The easiest way to make this preliminary trim is with a pair of scissors. Make sure that you leave about an inch on all sides beyond the size of the book.

Sometimes, depending upon the size of the book and the direction in which you have folded the paper, you can get two sets of flyleaves out of the same piece of paper.

What needs to be done at this point is to make a small shelf so that you can tip the free flyleaf onto the bulk of the pages of the book. Presuming that we are now putting in the front flyleaf, then you would tip the flyleaf onto the next page in the front of the book. An easy way to make this shelf is to place the folded edge of the flyleaf up against the edge of your work table, move it up about 3/16" and then press to make a soft crease parallel to the fold. This should have created a small shelf, on which you are going to put the adhesive. Look at the illustration to make sure you understand this, fig 7.

You should fit this into the book so that you can see how it is going to work before you put any adhesive on it. The little folded shelf is going to go down onto the next page in the book. The fold, of course, will go into the spine or hinge area. This will leave the open edges where they belong at the top, bottom, and fore-edge.

Apply a thin line of adhesive all along this little shelf and spread it out with a brush; the small, stiff oil brush works best for this. Make certain that you get any sloppy excess off, or it will cause trouble for you later.

Put the flyleaf back in the way you tried it out, with the folded edge well up into the hinge area and the shelf with the adhesive side down onto the next page. Put a folded piece of waxed paper right up to the edge of the glued area between the flyleaves and the next page down. This is to prevent the free flyleaf from sticking to the next page down at any point except the area of the small shelf, should any adhesive spread out when the book is put under pressure.

Run the folding bone or your fingernail firmly along the entire length of the back of this shelf to make certain that it is down securely and evenly.

Do both flyleaves in this manner and then put the book under weights or in the press for several hours to dry. In fact, leaving it overnight to be sure that it is dry will not hurt at all.

After the adhesive has dried, carefully remove the waxed paper. If you have used too much adhesive, the waxed paper may stick slightly, but if you ease it out carefully, it should come free.

The next step is to trim the flyleaf. This is probably the most crucial and the most exacting step you will have to do in any type of book repairing. If you don't do it properly, then it would be best to remove the flyleaf you have tipped in and start again from the beginning.

Two important things to watch here are that your knife blade is very, very sharp and that the bookboard you are going to cut into does not have too many ridges in it from previous uses that would makes your knife veer off its course.

It is important that you get all your elements carefully set up correctly before you do any cutting. See the illustration for a guide (fig. 8). The bottom layer is the cover of the book (in this case, the front cover, as we are talking about replacing the front flyleaf first). Next comes the bookboard scrap or whatever you are using in its place, then the front flyleaves which you are going to trim. Next you are going to place the flat metal ruler under the pages

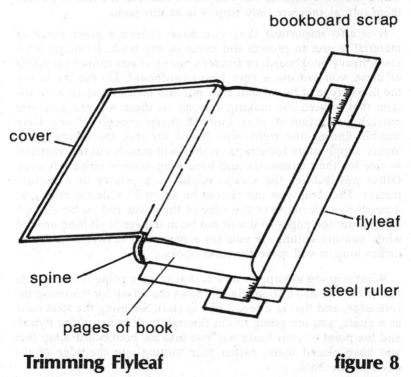

bookboard scrap

cover

flyleaf

spine

steel ruler

pages of book

Trimming Flyleaf   **figure 8**

of the book and right up the edge, as this is going to serve as a guide for you in cutting the flyleaves and it will also prevent the knife from going into the pages and nicking them. Your set-up should look exactly like the one in the illustration.

Leave the other cover folded back out of the way. If you are replacing both sets of flyleaves, you can either push the other ones back with the cover or work around them, which is what I prefer to do. One of the reasons for the preliminary trimming is so that you do not have a lot of excess paper that will get in your way. You can imagine what it would be like if you had three or four inches of paper left all the way around to get in your way while you were trying to trim the opposite set of flyleaves. Not only would they get in your way and perhaps throw your knife off while you were cutting, but you would also run the risk of pulling them out, as they are only tipped in at this point.

It is also important that you have chosen a good piece of material to use to protect the cover of the book. It should be a good, heavy bookboard, or binder's board; if you cannot get either of these, you can use a very heavy cardboard. Do not try to use the flimsy type of board that they put into men's shirts, or even the type that is used for making cartons, as these will not give you enough protection if your knife is sharp enough. If you have trouble finding the right type board for this, try asking at an artists' supply store for scraps, as they will usually cut this material to size for their customers and have long, narrow strips left over. Other possibilities for scraps might be a printer or a picture framer. The scrap you use should be about 3" wide (or more), as it needs to stick out over the edge of the cover and go far enough back under the pages so it will not be in danger of shifting around while you are cutting. If you get a piece that is twelve to fifteen inches long, it will serve for most books.

What is going to happen now is that you are going to make your first trim. The illustration (fig. 8) shows the set-up for trimming the fore-edge, and that is where I like to start. So, using the steel ruler as a guide, you are going to cut through both layers of the flyleaf, and the point of your knife will bite into the bookboard scrap that you have placed there, rather than cutting into the edge of the cover of the book.

When making the actual cut, you are going to have to press down on the bulk of the book very hard with the hand that is not doing the cutting. It is necessary to stand up and put the weight of your body behind it. You are now going to trim the fore-edges of the flyleaves to the size of the pages by bringing the knife down the length of the side, slowly and firmly. You will only get one go at this. There is very little chance if you mess it up that you can go back over it.

Once you get started making the cut, you should not stop for any reason; take it right through to the end. It will probably take some time before you feel confident at it; the first few times I attempted it, I had to hold my breath. Once you do master this technique, it will give you a great sense of satisfaction to see them trimmed off straight and even, just as they should be. I would not ever try to make this crucial cut with a pair of scissors, as I have seen one author advocate. What you want here is a very professional-looking cut, and the way I have outlined it is the best way to get that.

Now you will have to trim off the top or the bottom edge. Both of these have the potential of giving you more of a problem because the ruler that you are cutting against will not go all the way back to the spine. It will stop right at the edge of the area that you tipped in. There is nothing that you can do about this except be very careful at the beginning of the cut.

You must trim from the spine out toward the fore-edge, and not the other way about. This is very important, and has been talked about in connection with other operations in both cleaning and repairing. In this case, it is really essential, or you will most likely tear up the flyleaf as you are trying to trim it.

One of these edges is going to be very awkward to cut. If you are right-handed, it will be the bottom edge for the front flyleaf and the top edge for the back flyleaf. What is going to happen is that you are going to have to work "cross handed" in order to make the cut from the spine out to the fore-edge. This is not easy to explain, but you will see what happens when you try to do it. There is nothing you can do about, and you will just have to get used to this awkward position in order to make the cut properly.

This will also be the hardest cut to start because you will have two things working against you: the absence of the ruler as a guide for the very first part of the cut, and the "cross handed" position. I often find that I end up with a slight roughness right at the beginning where I did not have the ruler to guide me. This is easily corrected by opening up the book and snipping the rough area off to match the rest of the cut with a pair of sharp, pointed scissors.

When you have trimmed all three free edges of the top flyleaves, you should turn the book over and do the three edges of the bottom ones. Make certain that you place the board and the ruler carefully each time, before you make your trim. Also remember to press down hard on the rest of the book, and to make your cut slowly and firmly.

Now you are ready to glue down that part of the flyleaf that goes on the inside cover. Again, the first thing to do is to get "set up".

Place a flat piece of waxed paper between the two parts of the front flyleaves, as this is the one we are going to glue down first. This piece of waxed paper should extend an inch or more beyond all three open edges of the flyleaves and go right back into the hinge, up against the spine.

On top of this piece of waxed paper, you must place a piece of paper that also extends an inch or more beyond the three open edges of the flyleaves. This is what I use pages from an old telephone directory for. When I am working on very large books, I use more than one page when necessary. Any scrap paper that fills this need can be used, of course. Close the top part of the flyleaf down on the paper and waxed paper.

You are now going to apply the adhesive. For this, you will need a wide brush. The one I use is a 1" nylon trim painting brush for interior woodwork. I have cut the length of the bristles down to about an inch so that I have better control over it. If you leave the bristles long, they are too floppy, and since you are going to have to work very quickly, this could be a great problem for you. Each time, before you use this brush, make certain that the bristles are flexible. I usually push it down on my work table a couple of times to break up the bristles. There is nothing more frustrating than getting your brush full of adhesive, putting it down on the paper, and finding that it is as hard as a putty knife.

Another important thing is that you keep the adhesive you are going to use for this operation in a wide-mouth jar or a wide plastic container. I tried a couple of times to squeeze it out of an applicator onto the paper; not only is it too slow a process, but it comes out in a stream and leaves a ridge of adhesive, so you waste a lot of time dispersing it before you can really get down to work.

As I have pointed out, you are going to have to work fairly quickly once you start spreading the adhesive. The adhesive goes on the side of the flyleaf that is now uppermost, the side that is going to be glued down. It does not go on the inside cover. In this case, it is simply a matter of trust: this way works.

I like to make certain the spine area or hinge area has its share of adhesive, so I usually apply it down the length of the spine first. Then I start at the top and work down at a fast, steady pace, spreading the adhesive out from the spine to the edges. Be sure you go over all the edges out onto the page of telephone directory or other scrap paper you have inserted, which is what it is there for.

You must cover the entire flyleaf, and at the same time be careful not to get the adhesive on too thick or lumpy. Also, if you work too slowly, you will find that the edges of the flyleaf will start to curl under. this could cause problems if allowed to go too far. You should try to stay ahead of this by working fairly quickly.

When the entire area has adhesive spread on it, lift up the cover and let it drop down onto the glued surface!! Quickly press on the cover with the edge of your hand in a sliding motion, again working from the spine out to the edges. Press hard, and make certain that you go over the entire area. This too should be done fairly rapidly so that you cover the entire area; then, if you like, you can go back over it again.

Open the cover and you will now see the flyleaf glued in place. Remove the page from the telephone book or other scrap paper that you have used, and fold it so that the glued areas come together. Throw it away. Do not leave it lying around open or the first thing you know, you will put your arm down on it or, what is worse, you will set a book on it. Do not remove the piece of waxed paper; it should be clean, as the scrap paper should have taken care of all the adhesive.

If any of the adhesive has bled out onto the edges of the inside cover, you should clean it up right away with a clean rag or your finger. If you use your finger, wipe or wash it thoroughly so you don't spread any adhesive around inadvertently. If you have been careful not to get a lot of excess adhesive on the flyleaf in the first place, you should not have any trouble with adhesive coming out at this point. Also, if you have smoothed over the cover as you should have just after closing it on the adhesive, you should not have any ripples. Actually, this is the whole point of gluing in this manner: to avoid ripples and wrinkles in the flyleaf. I never have had more than the faintest ripple, and that only seldom.

This has always gone away as the book was drying under pressure. If you do this without a book press, then you will have to weight it down as securely as possible to avoid any problems of this sort and to avoid having the covers buckle due to the moisture in the adhesive.

You can now close the cover down onto the waxed paper. If any more adhesive comes out while the book is under pressure, the waxed paper will prevent it from doing any harm.

Turn the book over and glue down the back flyleaf in the same manner. Remember to get set up first, so you don't have to look for anything just when you need it, and remember to work quickly with the adhesive.

When you have finished, put the book in the press, with the two pieces of waxed paper in place, for about twelve hours. You must have a good, firm pressure so that the flyleaves dry evenly and flat, and so that there is no chance of the covers buckling.

The next step is to go and wash out your brushes with soap and water, and dry them off. It is really important to take care of your tools at the end of each operation or you will find that they get ruined and you will be in the middle of trying to do something, reach for a brush, and find that it is completely unusable.

After any major gluing operation, I like also to have a look at my work area and make certain that it is cleaned up. Adhesive has a way of getting in all sorts of places and if you don't get it cleaned up right away, it turns into a problem. At the same time, you have to make certain that your applicator container is tightly closed and that your wide-mouth jar or plastic container is sealed tightly; left open, the adhesive will dry out, and may even spoil.

If you find that you have any trouble with the adhesive sticking up the lid of the wide-mouth jar so that you have trouble getting it open, take a minute and clean all the adhesive out of the threads on both the jar and the cap. Hot water works really well in getting adhesive off. Then put a double layer of waxed paper between the lid and the jar. As this wears out and gets messy, you can just change it, and you won't have the sticking problem any longer.

After twelve hours, when the adhesive has had a chance to dry thoroughly, remove the book from the press, remove the waxed paper, and check to see that the hinges are flexible.

If all this sounds like a lot of work — it is! It takes a lot of practice and a lot of patience to do all these things in the right order. It takes even more patience to learn how to do them carefully and correctly, but once you have mastered the process, it should start to come pretty easily to you. I still have to be very careful when I am trimming; it is always a lesson in being precise. But there is a great deal of satisfaction in opening a book the next day, after it has dried, and seeing a new set of endpapers in place that look good.

MAINTAINING
YOUR LIBRARY

Your "Library" may be a shelf of books, or it may be a whole room set aside for the purpose. Whichever it is, how you maintain your library will largely determine how well your books will survive. Certainly, if you have any books of value, you will want to see that they are well cared for so they maintain that value and perhaps even increase it in time.

Bookshelves

Bookshelves should not be too crowded or the bindings will be damaged. Also, when you try to take a book out of a tightly packed shelf, the tendency is to pull at the top of the spine, which will cause damage very quickly.

Neither should they be too loose, because this too will damage the bindings. Books should stand upright and not be allowed to lean over, as this weakens them and causes bowed covers. If your shelves are too loose, you should use bookends to keep the books upright.

Large books and coffee-table type books should be laid down flat or, if you have some room in your gramophone record shelves, you might consider keeping them there in an upright position.

Periodicals are a very special case. They should be stored flat. If you have a number of these that you want to keep, I would suggest you look in the chapter on PROBLEMS in the section called "Periodicals".

It is best to keep your books toward the front of the shelves. This keeps them from coming in contact with the walls, from which they might pick up moisture, and at the same time allows air to circulate freely behind them.

Many people have romantic ideas about old bookshops with piles of books everywhere, and assume that this is a good way to keep their books. All I can say is, resist the temptation. Books can survive quite well in neat stacks for a while, but the tendency is to leave them there too long; they often get knocked over and then they get damaged. Also, the bottom books, in contact with the floor, can easily pick up moisture which could go unnoticed for a long period of time, and then you have a problem.

The best thing to do is to avoid stacking books at all, unless it is while you are cleaning the shelves.

Checking the Shelves

Once a year, or even every six months, you should take all your books off the bookshelves. The shelves should be thoroughly cleaned and cared for.

This is the time you can check over your books for the following problems:

  Sun-faded covers
  Moisture and mildew
  Excessive dryness
  Bugs and pests
  Torn dust jackets
  Damaged books

Those books that need to be repaired should be set aside and seen to following the methods you have learned in other parts of this book.

All the books should have the top edges vacuumed or dusted off. The covers, on books that have no dust jackets, should be dusted or brushed and waxed where necessary. It is an especially good idea to check over your leather-bound books, as these benefit from regular feeding with a good preservative followed by waxing.

Sun and Excessive Lighting

After you move to a new house or apartment, you should check through your books every few months to make certan that the sun is not getting to your shelves and making the books fade. In some places, the sun moves so drastically that it is just not possible to predict what will happen at a given season until you have been there a full year. If you do find fading, then you should move your books to a different spot or a different room. You should at the same time check for moisture.

Moisture and Mildew

If you do find moisture and mildew in your books, then you will have to take several steps to cure the problem. The books themselves can be dealt with as outlined in the chapter on PROBLEMS in the section on "Mildew".

A room dehumidifier or the dehumidifier crystals that are sold for mobile homes will often help a room that has moisture problems. If the moisture is coming in from an outside wall where you have shelves, you can put plastic on the wall behind the bookshelves. If it is your own house, you might consider insulating the walls where you are having problems with moisture. If you are not willing to do this, then you should find a different place to keep your books.

Mildew thrives in damp, stagnant places; therefore, one of the ways to prevent it is to air out your rooms whenever possible. It also likes warm places, so you should not keep your book areas around excessive heat.

Ideally, the temperature should be somewhere around 60° to 70° F. (about 19°C.) at all times, and the humidity should be around 50%. It is hard to maintain conditions like this unless you are running a library, but this gives you an idea of the ideal conditions.

I have heard that you can help prevent mildew by putting a few drops of oil of lavender on your book shelves. It certainly would not hurt to try, and it would make the area smell nice.

Excessive Dryness

The other side of the moisture and mildew problem is excessive dryness, because it will cause the bindings to crack and the paper to become brittle. I am sure you have at some time seen old newspapers or magazines that literally fall apart when you touch them. It is really bad when you find a book that is so dried out that it does this.

Not only are some climates very dry, but many people like to keep their houses excessively warm. Many heating systems literally pull the moisture right out of the air. Needless to say, books should not be kept right over a heating radiator.

If you find this sort of problem, you should do something to put some moisture back into the air. One of the easiest things to do is to put a dish of water on the heating radiator and make sure it stays filled up. You will probably be amazed at how fast it dries up. You can, of course, also get room humidifiers, which you might have to do in extreme cases or in very dry climates.

Bugs, Pests, etc.

Another major problem that you might run into is bugs. This usually means book lice (psocids) or silverfish. Both of these pests thrive in warm, damp rooms. If you find any evidence of bugs in your books, you should clean and air out your rooms. If you are having problems with dampness, then see the sections on "Moisture and Mildew".

You should also consider using an insecticide to get rid of them, and it would be wise to follow it up in a couple of weeks with another treatment, to catch any eggs that might hatch out.

Preventatives for bugs include pyrethrum powder (which is now used for getting rid of fleas on cats, so you can find it in the form of cat flea powder), camphor crystals, eucalyptus leaves, pennyroyal (a strong-smelling herb), and mothballs. Also, I have read that in the past people sometimes placed the leaves of an aromatic plant called costmary in their books to deter silverfish.

As for dealing with the books themselves when you have a bug problem, you should move all the bugs you actually see. Air the books out thoroughly and use an insecticide on them. Another method is to place the books in an enclosed box in which you have put mothball flakes. The books must be standing on end with the pages spread open, and you should leave them there for several days.

If you have problems with mice or cockroaches, you could try putting out mothballs, as apparently they do not like them, but this is, at best, only a temporary solution, and you had better consider doing something serious about the situation, like exterminating them.

Storing Books

If you find that you are going to have to store books away for any reason, there are several things that you should keep in mind.

Books should be packed carefully into cartons. If you are storing any paper items or oversize items, make sure that you pack them carefully so that they do not get damaged as you move the cartons.

It is a good idea to keep the cartons up off the floor so that dampness does not travel up into them. This can be solved by placing the bottom carton on a couple of pieces of 2 × 4 inch wood.

Make certain that the room or place you are storing them in is as free from dampness as possible and that there is a good circulation of air.

In any case, it is good to check through any books that you are storing, every three months or so, to make sure that they are not contracting any dampness or bugs. I certainly would not put it off any longer than that. It is a lot easier to clean up and prevent further problems if you catch them early than to do it once they have become well entrenched.

Another approach, and a very good one, is to take out some insurance against both moisture and bugs. Put some dehumidifier crystals and moth balls in each carton before you close it up. This does not, however, take the place of checking the cartons every three months, although it will be a help.

Storing Things in Books

It is not a very good idea to store things in books.

Bulky items will weaken the bindings of books and should not be kept in them. If you have items of this type that you want to go along with a book, then you should consider keeping them right next to the book, wrapped in a plastic wrap to keep them together.

Newspaper cuttings will turn brown in time and then they often stain the book. As these stains are almost impossible to remove, it is better to avoid them. If you feel that you want to store a newspaper cutting in a book, then put it in between two pieces of waxed paper.

Example of Catalogue Card

figure 9

Rhead, G. Wolliscroft. CHATS ON COSTUME. London, Unwin, 1906.
very good coverage and comments.
117 illustrations, photo and line drawings
historical by item of dress

Contents: Tunic
              Mantle
              Doublet and Hose
              Kirtle or Petticoat
              Rise and Fall of the Crinoline
              Collars and Cuffs
              Hats, Caps and Bonnets
              Dressing the Hair, Moustachios and Beard
              Boots, Shoes and other Coverings of the Feet

It is also not a good idea to press flowers into books, no matter how romantic it sounds. The reasons are the same as for newspaper cuttings, and the solution is the same, too.

If you find any of these things in books and need to do something about the problems they have caused, then look them up in the chapter on PROBLEMS. In the case of bulky items, you will have to look up what it has done, which probably is cracked the hinges.

Cataloguing

If you have a highly technical or a "working" library, you might want to consider cataloguing it. This sounds a lot more complicated than it is, really.

Basically, there are three ways to catalogue: by author, by title, or by subject. Whether you catalogue by author or by title depends primarily on how you relate to your books. If you think in terms of authors, then you will want to catalogue that way. If you think in terms of titles, then you will want to catalogue by that method. No matter which of these you choose, you still might want to have cards that tell you which books to consult for specific subjects.

I find that using 3 × 5 inch index cards is the easiest way to keep a cataloguing system for a library. Some of the information that you might want to include is:

    author
    title
    publisher
    date of publication
    comments
    contents

You may not find all of these necessary, but I would rather take a little more time in the beginning and put it all on the card than have to wonder, for example, what the contents were. Some people also like to include the date they got the book and the price they paid for it. I don't happen to find that type information necessary, so I do not include it.

For an example of what one of my catalogue cards might look like, see the example on the preceding page.

If I were then to make up subject cards, I would use cards of a different colour from the author or title index and list this particular book on a card titled "Costume". I probably would also list it on cards that pertained to areas where I had particular interests and would find myself doing research quite often; for example, if you have a subject card for "Hats", you list all of your books that contain information on hats on that one card (or run over to another if you need to). I am sure that you can see how helpful the subject cards are if you have to find books that contain information on a particular subject. In the case of your own library, all you would need to do would be to list the titles of all the books that had information on that particular subject, on the card.

Lending Books

Another advantage of using cards to catalogue your library is that if and when you lend a book, you can pull the card for the book and write on the back of it in pencil the following information:

Borrower's name
Address
Telephone number
Date borrowed

These cards should be kept aside, rather than filed back into the regular catalogue system. When the book comes back, then the pencilled information is erased before the card is returned to its place in the file.

If the book does not come back in a reasonable length of time, then you can follow it up from the information you have on the back of the card and remind the borrower that you "need it".

If you do not use a card system, then you should keep a list of the books you have out and include the same sort of information as listed above so that you can follow them up that way. Don't rely on your memory, as that is a good way to lose books.

As I have pointed out earlier, the number of times you write your name in a book will not determine whether it is returned to you or not. Some people are just very bad about returning books and others are not. There is really no way to be certain about this beforehand.

If you cannot bring yourself to ask for the book back, or if you have lent it to someone you hardly know and cannot trace, then you deserve to lose it!

Another way to approach this problem is look straight in the eye at anyone who asks you if they can borrow a book, and say, "I am sorry, but I never lend books." That might have an initial bad reaction, but it will probably save you a lot of grief in the long run.

REPAIRING BOOKS
FOR LIBRARIES

About a year ago, I started to repair books for our small local lending library. At first, I approached this in exactly the same way I would have if I had been repairing books for an art museum or for my own purposes. I soon found that this was not what was needed.

There are many types of libraries, which not only serve different purposes, but also regard and use their books in different ways. Museum libraries usually have books on specialized subjects and are mainly for researchers, although some of them are open to the public for reference. Corporate or business libraries are in most cases even more specialized and are not usually open to the public at all. Lending libraries in general have newer books, geneyal reference works, and not usually anything that would be considered very valuable. Large, well endowed libraries and university libraries often span the gap between the other types of libraries and have collections of very rare books (often under lock and key) as well as having a large number of books that are lent out.

When you start to clean and repair books for someone else, the first thing you have to determine is what is important to them. We have so far talked a lot about making books last and not destroying their value. We have been concerned with preserving books without being too technical about it. As I have said before, if you are dealing with really valuable books, then it is best to let an expert handle them; it is certainly worth the money that you will be charged to have it done properly. In the meantime, you might decide to improve your knowledge of the subject by taking a good bookbinding course so that you can in time take over some of this work. When you are repairing or cleaning books for yourself or for a reference library, you want to do the best job possible and make the books last; but I have found that the main concern of a lending library is to keep books in circulation as long as possible so that they will not have to be replaced. This may sound like a short-term goal, but lending libraries are mainly concerned with newer books, many of which will be discarded when no longer popular, so that their attitude is entirely different, in many ways, from the attitude you would have in terms of your own books, and certainly very different from the concerns you would have for rare and really valuable books. I found I could understand this emphasis on keeping books in circulation without the need to preserve them for the future, and work within that context even though it was contrary to my usual way of working.

The first stumbling block that I needed to get over was the fact that libraries must mark their books in various ways both for identification and to help in finding and re-shelving the books within their system. This takes the form of numbers on the spine; bookmarks, rubber stamps, addresses or impression stamps on the inside and often on the top edge; and, in the case of lending libraries, pockets for the issue cards, etc.

On the other hand, library books do not seem to have a lot of marks put in them by the borrowers, probably because they are not kept out long enough to be referred back to, and so there is less temptation for underlining or comments to be written in. Therefore, many of the internal cleaning problems that one finds with used books will not occur. Oftentimes, there are soiled covers and these will have to be dealt with in the usual manner; but basically the problem is one of wear and tear, which shows up in split hinges and, especially with recently published books, in whole sections separating from the binding. When you are dealing with hardbound books, the best thing you can do is to follow the instructions that I have given previously and get the books back into usable condition so that they can be returned to the shelves.

Many of the problems I was not prepared for came up with children's books and, to a lesser extent, with paperbound books.

Both these types of books seem to be programmed to self-destruct after being read one or two times; this is, of course, not the intent of the library. Aside from the internal damage problems, which are the same as I have mentioned above with regard to hardbound books, there is the added difficulty of the outer spine giving way. The solution to this problem was already being used by the librarian and staff in another way. They had always put the library numbers on the spine of this type book with a label which was then secured with transparent tape. The result was that the spine would tear and come apart everywhere except that portion where the tape had been applied. So the solution was to put the tape all along the outer spine to start with, and it works very well. this tape is a plastic-based transparent tape, and the type we use is about two to three inches wide.

If your reaction to this is "but you said never use transparent tape on a book", you are absolutely right, and I would normally stand by that, but in this case, the books have a limited life and the object is to ensure that they remain in circulation as long as possible. Therefore, we are faced with a situation where an otherwise unacceptable method achieves the ends we must have, and it should be used. This book tape is also very effective for reinforcing the outer spines of paperbound books, and books with covers of what are known as "papercovered boards", these latter usually being children's books or, sometimes, craft books.

I also found that the library had been using this same tape when trying to repair hinges that had cracked on hardbound books (and sometimes even larger paperbound books), and the results were anything but good. What happened in this instance was that, ultimately, the repair held, to the detriment of the rest of the book. The repaired area was so strong that the other parts of the book tended to pull away from the spine to compensate. In this case, the use of book tape was very wrong. As it was not possible to remove the tape without great damage to the book, I had to cut through it and then fix the hinge in the usual way (with adhesive). The result can never be wholly satisfactory, as the tape cannot be removed; but at least the book ends up in better shape and stronger, and will hold together longer.

Another point I would make about mending books for libraries is that, since you know that they are going to receive a lot more wear and tear than books you would repair for yourself at home, you can be a little more generous in applying adhesive to the cracked hinges or sections pulling loose. The main result you want to achieve is strength, for the stronger the books are, the longer they will stay in circulation. Also, a good coat of book wax on the covers will help ensure that hardbound books last longer and suffer less from excessive handling.

You may recall from the instructions on how to put back loose pages or loose sections that usually it will be necessary to trim a bit off the pages to make them fit back properly. This really is necessary when you are dealing with any book that is to be kept, but in the case of general circulation library books, it becomes a question of whether or not it is worth the time involved. We found that it was still a good idea on most hardbound books, but not really worth the effort on most paperbound books where whole sections were pulling out, as they are not going to last long anyway. This is the sort of decision that you will have to make on the spot and in conjunction with the librarian.

Again, let me stress that we are talking about ordinary books that the library has on the shelves for general circulation. You certainly would not treat long-term reference books, books in special collections, or any other book that has a long-term life in this manner. What you must determine from the outset is what type book you are being asked to repair and what the purpose of that book is. If you do these things, you cannot go wrong in seeing that the books fulfill their functions.

There are special supplies available to libraries, but libraries which can afford them usually have a special repair department or their own bindery. Smaller libraries will sometimes find a few of these supplies suit their purposes and it does not require extensive equipment and personnel to be able to use them.

The library staff would do well to study the chapter entitled MAINTAINING YOUR LIBRARY to make certain that the proper attention is being paid to the books on the shelves. Remember, it is far easier to catch a problem while it is still small, and deal with it then, than it is to wait until the book is literally falling apart and wonder what to do about it at that point. Proper library maintenance is the key to keeping your books in good repair, and that is true whether we are considering books in the lending library or books in your home. It would be a very good idea to establish a schedule to make certain not only that the shelves are cleaned at regular intervals, but also that the books are checked, section by section, and if nothing else that the covers are waxed once or twice a year; at the same time, any books in really bad shape can be pulled out for repairs.

This may sound like quite an undertaking when you think of the library as a whole, but it will save you work and save the library a lot of money in the long run. If the work is done piecemeal, so that a different area is checked each week, then the maintenance becomes much easier to deal with and does not seem so overpowering. Also, it is mandatory that books be checked for damage when they come back from borrowers, so that they will not be put back on the shelves until they have been repaired. This is probably the most critical spot in the whole library system, as it is the easiest place to spot a damaged book at a point where it must be handled in any case.

By establishing these routines, you will find that after a short time your library will be in good order and that you have cut down on the amount of repairs needed by discovering them early.

"DON'TS" —
A REVIEW SECTION

This chapter is really a form of review and should also serve as a reinforcement of some basic ideas.

It is true that many books have survived for hundreds of years, but think of the many, many more that are lost to us because they were not properly cared for. I remember going into a secondhand shop in London recently and going into a back room where they had hundreds of books on a great variety of subject. All of these books were somewhere between 75 and 150 years old, and without exception they were falling apart. I was horrified.

So, even though this is not a book about the conservation of rare books, I think that it is the intent of everyone who works with books to try to preserve them for future generations to enjoy.

With this in mind, I have prepared a list of "Don'ts";

Don't do anything that will damage a book

Don't do any repairs that cannot be undone

Don't try to repair old and valuable books unless you are an expert

Don't expect all books to react well to the same treatment; each book should be treated as an individual

Don't try something that is beyond your skill, unless you are working on a "practice book".

Don't try new products on a good book until you have some experience with them on a "practice book"

Don't work on the inside covers without a support underneath

Don't use cloth tape to fix the spine of a book

Don't write your name all over your books; once is enough

Don't wash the covers of a book

Don't get books wet

Don't set beverages, hot or cold, on books

Don't leave your books lying around in stacks

Don't use rubber bands to keep a book together

Don't ever erase coloured pages without testing them first

Don't do anything to coloured pages without testing them first

Don't use "Scotch"-type tape on books

Don't treat suede bindings like smooth leather bindings

Don't store bulky things in books

Don't keep newspaper cuttings in books unless between waxed paper

Don't press flowers in books unless between waxed paper

Don't use rubber stamps to mark books

Don't use marking pens in books

Don't use paperclips in books

Don't use rubber cement to make repairs

Don't store books in damp rooms

Don't expose books to strong light or to sunlight for long periods of time

Don't keep books in extremely dry conditions or over a heat radiator

Don't ever trim flyleaves toward the spine; always work from the spine out the fore-edge

Don't forget to put waxed paper protection sheets in when you are working with adhesive

Don't be in a hurry; take your time when you are repairing books, unless you are working with adhesive

Don't use inferior materials when repairing books

Don't pack your bookshelves too tightly

Don't allow your books to flop around in the shelves

Don't forget to maintain your library properly

Don't forget to check stored books every three months for both moisture and bugs

Don't forget to clean your books and bookshelves thoroughly at least once a year

PACKING AND
POSTING BOOKS

It has been suggested to me that I say a few words on packing and posting books, since I do so much of that. This may not be an immediate problem for you, but soon or later we all have to deal with it.

Wrapping Books

It really amazes me that many people, who take very good care of their books, feel that once a book is to be sent to someone else (usually because it has been sold) they have lost all responsibility for it. What usually happens is that the book gets shoved into a padded book bag or, what is worse, several books get dumped into a box, and off it goes to the post office. Sometimes people do not even put a return address on the package, as if they were saying "I don't ever want to see this again."

The results of this kind of mistreatment are that the books arrive with the covers scraped and, in extreme cases, torn. I have even seen books that have had enough room to open up in the carton and things have slipped in and the pages have torn. It is easy to avoid this, even if it does take an extra couple of minutes.

If you have to send a regular-sized book to anyone, then padded or air-bubble book bags are just fine. However, I would not put a book into anything without wrapping it first. I use newspaper unless the cover of the book is very light and there is a danger of the newsprint coming off on it. I also fix the ends of my wrapping down with masking tape, or "Scotch"-type tape, to prevent the book from sliding out and getting damaged. Sometimes you can even send two books in a padded bag if they are about the same size. Either wrap them together or tape the two books, which are wrapped separately, together.

If I have several books to send, I usually use a carton to post them in. Sometimes I take a larger carton and cut it down to the size I need. Again, I wrap the books individually in newspaper and seal these parcels up. Or, in some cases, I will wrap two books of the same size together.

I always use a rubber stamp with my name and address to mark each of these newspaper-wrapped books. This is in case something should happen to the package and it should be torn open, I would still have a chance of getting the books back. Return address stickers will also work, and of course if you seldom send books and don't have these things, then writing it on will work, too.

You should also make certain that your package is secure and that things do not rattle around. In the case of book bags, this is fairly easy: if you do not have a lot of room left, a piece of crumpled newspaper will usually take care of that. When it comes to cartons, it can be a bit more work. In the first place, you should not use too much newspaper, as it is heavy. If you do use it for stuffing, then crumple it up. I usually use empty egg cartons for the big spaces, as they are sturdy and light, and take up a lot of room. I also use those "plastic peanuts", the polystyrene foam pellets, to fill in small spaces.

When I am sending a carton, I put a piece of cardboard on top of everything as a final touch, so that if the person opening the package uses a knife the books will not be cut into.

If you are sending flimsy paper items or periodicals in a padded book bag, you should put them on a piece of cardboard first and then wrap the whole thing in newspaper before putting it in the bag. It is very easy for flimsy items to get damaged.

It is wise to use corner protectors on any books that are expensive or rare. They are also sometimes necessary if the corners of the book being sent show any wear or might be fragile. There is detailed information on these in the chapter on PROBLEMS, including how to make your own.

Keep in mind that you want your books to arrive at the other end in the best possible condition.

Book bags should be sealed up by stapling the flap shut. You can then use masking tape to go over the staples so that they will not come out.

Cartons should be taped shut. I use brown, gummed tape which not only is strong but also covers up things on the outside of the carton that I do not want to show or that might confuse the post office. Then, after I have finished with that, I use a type of nylon strapping tape. I usually put this completely around the package in at least two directions. This makes a good, strong parcel.

I would suggest that you insure any package that is worth any great amount, as the post office is not known for getting better every year. Another approach is to mark your packages "BOOKS" on every side and very clearly, to help prevent theft. Usually, the people who steal from the mails are looking for things that are more valuable to them than books.

Also make certain that the name and address, including postal code, of the recipient is clearly marked: and remember to put your return address on all packages.

International Parcels

If you are sending parcels to any country in the Postal Union, which covers a good many countries, there are a few rules you should know.

Maximum weight is 5 kilos, or 11 pounds.
One end must be "unsealed".
Parcels usually cannot be insured.

The rule about being "unsealed" is to allow Customs inspectors to open the package if they need to. "Unsealed" does not mean "open".

If you are using a padded book bag, you are allowed two metal fasteners of the type with two prongs that you push through and fold back sometimes through a washer.

If you are sending a parcel, you should tuck in one end and not use any kind of tape on it although it is closed up. Then you have to use cord to tie the package securely. If the post office says anything, remind them that one end has to be unsealed and that tying it up is the only way you can make a secure package. You can't insure it anyway, so there is nothing they can do about it.

International parcels should be marked "Books" and should also be marked "Printed Matter at Reduced Rates". This latter is to satisfy the requirements of foreign postal systems.

FURTHER READING

The following books and pamphlets would be useful further reading. Those marked with an asterisk are reported in print at the time when this is written. Most of the others can probably be borrowed from your local library.

ARMITAGE *(F. D.): Causes of Mildew on Books and Methods of Protection* Bulletin No. 8. 1949 (P.A.T.R.A.)

BARROW (W. J.): *Manuscripts and Documents: their Deterioration and Restoration.* 1955. (University of Virginia Press).

BAYNES-COPE (A. D.): *Caring for Books and Documents,* 32pp. 1981. (British Museum).*

CLARK (J.): *The Care of Books.* An essay on the development of Libraries and their fiittings from the earliest times to the end of the 18th century. 1976. (Gordon Press).

COCKERELL (Douglas): *Bookbinding and the Care of Books.* Paperback. 1978 (Pitman).*

COCKERELL (Sydney M.): *The Repairing of Books.* 1958 (Sheppard Press).

ELLIS (Roger): *The Principles of Archive Repair.* 1951 (London School of Printing and Graphic Arts).

FOWLER (G. H.): *Care of County Muniments.* 1923 (The County Councils Association).

GRASS (H.): *Simplified Bookbinding.* 1976 (Scribner).

HORTON (Carolyn): *Cleaning and Preserving Bindings and Related Materials.* 1969 (American Library Association).*

KAFKA (Francis) *How to Clothbind a Paperback Book.* 1980 (Dover).*

LANGWILL (William Herbert): *The Conservation of Books and Documents.* 1957 (Pitman).*

MIDDLETON (Bernard): *The Restoration of Leather Bindings.* 1972 (American Library Association).*

MUIR (David): *Binding and Repairing Books by Hand.* 1978 (Arco).

PLENDERLEITH (H. J.): *The Preservation of Leather Bookbindings.* 1947 (British Museum).

WATSON (A.): *Hand Bookbinding.* 1963 (Bell).

YOUNG (Laura S.): *Bookbinding and Conservation by Hand: a Working Guide.* 1981 (Bowker Publishing Company.*

INDEX

Please note: Looking up specific things in the Index will not help you if you cannot do the basic operations as discussed in the chapter on Techniques.

Adhesive. 12, 13, 77
Bandage 12, 50, 63
Bleaching agents. 27, 58
Blunt knife. 12, 13
Book bags 94
Bookbinding 87
Book lice 81
Book plates 23, 26, 37
Book press. 12, 15
Book shelves 78
Brushes. 12, 14, 76
Bugs 81
Camphor crystals 81
Candle wax 38
Catalogue cards 83
Chewing gum 38
Chloramine T 27, 44, 46, 60
Cleaning solvent. 14
Coffee stains 41
Coloured paper. 24, 39
Cornflour paste. 13
Costmary 81
Cover dirt 42, 88
Cover fade. 32, 39
Cover spots 33, 39
Cover stains. 42
Covers detached 40
Covers dull 32, 40
Cracked hinges 28
Crayon 40
Cup rings 41
Cutting knife 12, 16
Dealer name sticker. 41
Dehumidifier crystals. 80
Denatured alcohol 48
Diatomaceous earth 48
Dirt on pages 41
Domestic parcels. 94
Dryness. 81
Dirty edges 30, 42
Dust jacket. 11, 42
Dusty covers 42, 88
Edges, dusty or dirty 30, 42
Edges, writing or rubber stamp
. . . . 43
Erasing 24, 48
Eucalyptus leaves 81
Flour paste 13
Flowers, pressed in. 43, 84
Fly stains 46
Flyleaves, replaced. 67
Folded-down corners 43
Foxing 44
Glass rings. 41
Glue stick. 12, 51
Grease 44
Grease pencil marks 40
Hexane. 14, 59
Hinges, cracked. 28

Hinges, loose but not cracked
.... 28, 44
Holes in pages............... 45
Hydrogen peroxide........ 48, 58
Ink eradicator 26
Ink underlining.............. 53
Ink marks & names......... 46
Insect stains................ 46
Insuring books 96
International parcels 96
Leather bindings............. 46
Leather preserver 16, 46
Leather wax................. 16
Leaves pressed in........... 43
Lemon juice................. 48
Lending books 85
Library numbers on spine..... 47
Liquid paper...... 12, 14, 26, 59
Marking pen 27, 47
Mildew.......... 14, 48, 65, 80
Moisture.................. 79, 80
Mothballs................... 81
Name on flyleaf 25, 49
Names & dates.............. 85
Name stickers 96
Newspaper cuttings 49, 83
Oil of lavender 80
Outer spine coming off 50
Oxalic acid................. 27
Paint on cover............... 51
Paperbacks................. 89
Paperback, section coming out. 51
Paperback, spine pulling away. 52
Paperclips.................. 53
Paper for flyleaves 67, 68
Paper separating............. 53
Pencil marks 27
Pencil underlining 27, 53
Pennyroyal................. 81
Periodicals 54, 78
Plates, book or presentation
.... 23, 26
Plates (illustration), loose 54

Potassium permanganate
.... 26, 41, 58
Post office................... 94
Practice books............... 22
Price on dust jacket 55
Price on flyleaf 24
Price stickers 55
Printed & decorated flyleaves.. 56
Psocids 81
Protecting corners........ 56, 95
Pyrethrum powder 81
Renaissance Wax 12, 16, 34
Replace flyleaves 67
Return address stickers 94
Rice paper........ 39, 45, 54, 61
Rubber cement........ 12, 40, 57
Rubber cement thinner 14, 57
Rubber stamp marks 58
Rust stains............... 53, 58
Sanding 25, 37
"Scotch"-type tape 58
Sections coming out.......... 58
Silverfish................... 81
Spine cracking, internal.... 28, 44
Stains 32, 58
Storing books 82
Stretch bandage 12, 50, 63
Suede bindings 60
Sun-faded covers 33, 60, 80
Tape, adhesive transparent
.... 12, 58, 59
Tape, cloth.............. 51, 60
Tea stains................... 59
Tears in covers 61, 66
Tears in pages............... 61
Thin spots on pages.......... 62
Thymol.................. 14, 48
Top edges dirty.............. 30
Top of spine damage......... 63
Torn dust jacket 11, 42
Trimming flyleaves........... 70
Underlining.............. 27, 45
Vellum bindings............. 64

Washed covers 32, 64
Water 65
Water-colour dyes 33, 39
Water stains................ 65
Waxing covers.............. 34

Wet books 48, 65
White bread.............. 32, 41
Wine stains 41, 59
Wrapping books 94